SHARE OUR WORLD

Share Our World

*a collection of multi-faith fables
for the primary school assembly*

Jeanne L. Jackson

SIMON & SCHUSTER
EDUCATION

First published in the United Kingdom in 1994 by
Simon & Schuster Education
Campus 400, Maylands Avenue
Hemel Hempstead, Herts HP2 7EZ

A catalogue record for this book is available from the British
Library

ISBN 0 7501 0522 4

Photoset by
Derek Doyle & Associates, Mold, Clwyd
Printed in the United Kingdom by
T.J. Press, Padstow

for Anthony
As-Salaam-Alaikum
May we share our world in peace.

Acknowledgements

Thank you …

to the staff and children of Cobden Primary School, who continue to be
a source of inspiration and joy.

Thank you …

Val, for your patient (!) support and understanding whilst this book was
in the making. Thank you also for your help in researching the material.

The Apostles' Creed is taken from the Book of Common Prayer, the
rights of which are invested in the Crown, and is reproduced by
permission of the Crown's Patentee, Cambridge University Press.

Contents

Introduction

Share our World is a collection of fables, gathered from our world's major religious backgrounds, adapted and retold to suit the primary school audience of today.

The original stories, with their direct and straight-forward action and language, held inner meanings beyond the literal and were not intended specifically for children. Professional story tellers narrated their tales to groups of people gathered together round camp fires or in communal places. The stories were passed on by word of mouth from one generation to the next. Many of the stories inevitably changed a little in retelling over time, as new elements were added and changes made to suit new audiences. It is in this tradition that *Share our World* is written. I have attempted to remain true to the original stories, whilst adapting them to suit today's primary school children.

The stories retell easily to large or small groups of children, and are therefore suitable for the large school assembly or for the classroom. In the latter, it is of course easier to elicit debate and discussion about the meanings behind the fables, to help children explore and communicate their own feelings and those of others, and to discuss particular courses of action in the stories and the consequences of those actions. However, it is possible to draw out the above points in a full assembly, perhaps with opportunity later for children to further discuss particular issues.

Why fables?

Fables are lively, exciting stories which reflect our various cultures' attitudes to life. Fables have a strong narrative, and are stories in which animals, insects or birds speak and behave like human beings, whilst retaining their inherent characteristics. This personification can extend to rivers, winds, trees, rocks and other natural objects. Fables animate the inanimate!

Fables, however, differ from other fictional tales, legends and myths in that a moral – a rule of behaviour – is woven into the story itself and forms an integral part of the whole.

Fables, therefore, are simple allegorical tales, constructed in such a way as to encourage the listener to search for meanings hidden beneath the literal surface. As such they are ideally suited to primary school assembly, with its mixed ages and abilities, since the stories can be enjoyed at a superficial level or plumbed for deeper meaning.

The fables in *Share our World* include several stories which are technically parables and myths. Parables, which are also allegorical tales, were used to pass down traditional folk wisdom, but where fables use animals to convey their messages, parables use people. Parables tend to concentrate less on the action of the story and more on the parallels drawn between certain aspects of human behaviour. Myths are narratives usually involving forces difficult to explain and understand. They are people's early attempts to explain the world in which they lived; to account for natural or social phenomena, and to explain the world's mysteries. Myths personify the earth and sky, the natural wonders and powers of the world, and as such are also allegorical tales.

The word fable comes from the latin *fabula*, meaning a telling. Fables emphasise the narrative and are traditionally short and to the point, but their origins are lost in history. The western fable begins effectively with Aesop (see page 144). The earliest surviving collection of Aesop's fables dates from the first century CE. It is believed that a book belonging to Alfred the Great (now lost) introduced the fables to England. In 1484 Caxton printed *The Boke of Subtyl Historyes and Fables of Esop*, and throughout the 15th and 16th centuries new versions of the fables were published. This number of different versions shows the regard in which the fables were held.

In the Middle Ages in Europe, fable – together with all other forms of allegory – was seen as a means of freedom and expression under conditions of strong social restraint. Medieval fable gave rise to lengthier stories known as beast epics. These were involved and complicated animal stories which mocked epic grandeur. The most famous of these were the 12th century related group of stories known as *Roman de Renart* (Reynard the Fox), which symbolised human cunning. Included in this group is the story of The Fox and the Chanticleer, which Chaucer used as the basis for his 'Nun's Priest's Tale'.

The writing of fables reached its height in late 17th century France, with the works of Jean de la Fontaine (see page 144). More recent fabulists include Hans Anderson, Lewis Carroll, Rudyard Kipling, George Orwell, Robert Louis Stevenson, James Thurber, J.R.R. Tolkein, and Oscar Wilde (see also page 145).

In India, fables appear in very early literature, and there is some argument as to whether the Hindu *Panchatantra* or the Buddhist *Jataka Tales* came first. It would certainly seem that many Aesopian fables of the west are derived from Indian sources, and several have been traced back, along various routes and in various ways, to the Jatakas (see also page 10).

The *Jataka Tales* are birth stories of the Buddha, and tell of some of his experiences in previous lives. Each story has a moral, and it is believed that the Jatakas show fable, for the first time, being used as a vehicle of instruction. The *Jataka Tales* may date from the 5th Century BCE, although written versions appeared much later than this.

The *Panchatantra*, believed by some to be the most important and complete compilation of folk stories in the world, is a collection of animal fables. The original was written in Sanskrit, was translated into Pahlavi, then emerged, translated again, as the Arabic *Kalilah wa Dimnah* in the mid 8th century (see also page 48). Unfortunately, both the original and its first translation are now lost.

Kalilah and Dimnah were two jackals who were the lion king's counsellors. The collection of stories is in fact a single story (frame story), which contains fables – some of these are in themselves frame stories – designed to teach wisdom and cunning. Care should be taken in their use with children, since the stories praise shrewdness, political cunning and worldly wisdom. The morals of some of the stories can be seen, within the context of today's society, as immoral

The *Fables of Bidpai* – the English title of the Kalilah and Dimnah stories – differ from the fables of Aesop in that the animals behave as men, but in animal form. They do not retain animal characteristics and modes of behaviour, as they do generally in Aesop.

The *Fables of Bidpai* were translated into many languages, including Hebrew, and later, Latin. It was through them that eastern fable was first introduced to Europe.

In China, around the 2nd century BCE, philosophers frequently used extended metaphors. Fable is the logical development of this, but its growth was impeded by the Chinese view that animals should not think and behave as human beings. The Chinese also believed that fact was more useful and instructive than fiction, which explains the development of the large number of Chinese legendary stories. These stories, although embroidered and extended as are most legends, were based on actual historical events.

However, between the 4th and 6th centuries CE, fables from Buddhist India were adapted by Chinese Buddhists, in a work known as *Po-Yu Ching*.

In Japan, the *Koji-Ki* and *Nihon-Shoki* ('Records of Ancient Matters' and 'Chronicles of Japan', recorded in the early and mid 8th century CE respectively), are official histories containing many fables. A recurring theme is that of a small insignificant animal gaining power over, or getting the better of, a larger, stronger creature.

Japanese fable writing reached its peak in the 13th century. During the 15th and 16th centuries, Aesop's fables were introduced to Japan by Jesuit missionaries, and influenced subsequent fabulists.

And so it can be seen that the history of fable, like fable itself, has its threads so closely interwoven that they are almost impossible to unravel. It can also be seen that not only are the threads closely interwoven, they are themselves in many cases very similar. We perceive our cultures, societies and religions to be so very different from each other, yet here, in these stories, we see the same themes recurring again and again. The story-tellers of the original fables used the tales to teach a point of conduct, a moral code for living. These stories are as relevant today as then. They are not confined to a particular time, place or civilisation. They are useful though not mundane, true whilst not being real. They are universal stories which can hopefully be enjoyed by everyone, whatever their background.

The stories form a colourful and sparkling fabric, woven from multi-ethnic threads. They are stories to share, so that we might all share our world.

Principal dates and people in the history of fable

8th century BCE. Hesiod, a Greek poet, is believed to have written a fable 'The hawk and the nightingale'.

5th century BCE. The *Jataka Tales* are believed to have come into existence in oral form.

2nd century BCE. Chinese philosophers make use of the extended metaphor.

620 – 560 BCE. The history of western fable effectively begins with Aesop, believed to have been a disabled Greek slave living in Phrygia.

1st century CE. Believed earliest surviving collection of Aesop's fables.

3rd century. Babrius, a Roman fabulist who lives in Syria.

4th – 6th centuries. Fables from Buddhist India are adapted by Chinese Buddhists. The work is known as *Po-Yu Ching*.

Early and mid 8th century respectively. In Japan, the *Koji-Ki* and the *Nihon-Shoki* ('Records of Ancient Matters' and 'Chronicles of Japan'), are recorded. The works contain many fables.

8th century. The *Panchatantra* is translated from the Pahlavi version into Arabic. It is known as 'Kalilah wa Dimnah' or 'The Fables of Bidpai'.

10th century. A collection of fables, entitled *Romulus*, is written in prose. Until now it has been the custom to write all fables in verse.

A version of the work of Phaedrus of Augustus is written in prose and used as a model by medieval fabulists. (Phaedrus of Augustus, in the reign of Tiberius, translated Aesop's verses into Latin prose, adding anecdotes of his own.)

12th century. The Beast Epic known as *Roman de Renart* written in France.

12th century (late). A notable collection of fables is made by Marie de France.

13th century. Japanese fable writing reaches its peak.

1484. Caxton prints *The Boke of Subtyl Historyes and Fables of Esop* in England.

15th – 16th centuries. Jesuit missionaries introduce Aesop's fables to Japan.

The work influences later fabulists.

1621 – 1695. Jean de la Fontaine is reputed to be the greatest fabulist of modern Europe.

Mid 17th century. Fable writing reaches its zenith in France.

1651 – 1715. The French writer Fenelon writes a book of fables to teach a royal prince his duties.

19th and 20th centuries. Fable finds a new audience with the advent of literature written specifically for children. Allegory rises in popularity as many authors investigate the medium, writing for adults and children.

1947. George Orwell writes *Animal Farm*, one of the most popular allegorical tales of modern times.

Assemblies and the Education Reform Act

The 1988 Education Reform Act raised much debate about school collective worship. A great deal of the hubbub has now died down, as schools have come to terms with the requirements of the Act, and have made, and are reviewing, their organisational arrangements for collective worship.

However, I feel it will be useful to reflect briefly on the 'collectivity' of school worship; the 'worship' aspect of assembly; and the style and character of worship in county schools.

The 1988 Act, like the 1944 Education Act, uses the term 'collective worship' and not 'corporate worship'; acknowledging that the worship must be appropriate to the assembly of people, not all of whom will be from the same religious, or indeed any religious, background. This places the school assembly in a uniquely challenging position. Where else would one find a large group of people from differing cultural and religious backgrounds in a situation of worship?

Worship, within the primary school, has a very broad outline. There is no single simple definition of the word, it has a range of meanings. On the one hand, worship can be the reverence paid to a Supreme Being by believers; on the other it can be a recognition of merit, of worth-ship; a celebration of the highest achievements of the human spirit. School assembly usually has some of the qualities of worship within it, and draws from a tradition of worship, but as with all elements of school life, children will approach it via different stepping stones; some will be used to joining in worship within their faith communities, others will never have experienced this but will be approaching worship for the first time through the school assembly.

The 1988 Act states that for County schools, the *majority* of acts of collective worship each term should be 'wholly or mainly of a broadly Christian character'. Those acts which are broadly Christian should reflect the 'broad traditions of

Christian belief without being distinctive of any particular Christian denomination'. The Secretary of State in DES Circular 3/89 (January 1989) gives greater flexibility in paragraph 34 by saying, 'An act of worship which is "broadly Christian" need not contain only Christian material provided that, taken as a whole, it reflects the traditions of Christian belief'.

It can be seen then that the provisions for collective worship can be interpreted in a broad and flexible way. School worship, which is part of the whole curriculum and intended to be an educational experience, can be presented sensitively to children of all faiths. No-one needs to be made to worship compulsorily in a way that is unacceptable to them.

The wording of the Act makes it possible for acts of worship to take place within schools which are not 'broadly Christian'. It allows for multi-faith acts of worship to take place, as long as the majority of acts of worship in any term are 'broadly Christian'. There is thus an enormous amount of flexibility built into the normal situation, as envisaged by the 1988 Education Reform Act.

Further reading

The Act Unpacked John M Hull (Christian Education Movement 1989)
The Education Reform Act 1988 (HMSO)
School Worship Bill Gent (Christian Education Movement 1989)

Buddhism

It is difficult to estimate the total number of Buddhists in the world today. Religious conditions in China, Tibet and Japan are unclear, but the general estimate is that there are some 200 million Buddhists worldwide, excluding those in China. It is believed there could be up to double this number within China, bringing the total number closer to 600 million. An estimated 100,000 Buddhists live in Great Britain.

Buddhist teaching has been known in the countries of the Far East for over 1500 years, but it is relatively new to European countries. Increased opportunities for travel, together with the work of translators and scholars, brought Buddhism to Britain in the late 19th and early 20th centuries. Further communication between east and west arose after recent conflicts: soldiers returning from serving in south-east Asia at the end of the Second World War brought Buddhist ideas back home; Tibetans who fled their country after the Chinese invasion of 1959, together with Vietnamese people who settled in Britain following the wars in Indo-China in the '50s and '60s, brought Buddhist beliefs and set up Buddhist Centres.

Buddhism has been described as a religion without a God. The Buddha (the word means Enlightened One, or Awakened One), is believed to have been born in India, about 563 BCE, as Prince Siddhartha Gautama. Siddhartha gave up his life of luxury and ease, and became a pauper in order to discover the meaning of life. After he had become 'Enlightened' or 'Awakened' he was given the title Buddha. Before that time he was known as the Bodhissatva – one capable of becoming enlightened.

Buddhists believe that the Buddha discovered Dharma, the truth about the way things are. They believe that the truth – not the person – is the underlying principle of Buddhism.

The Buddha's first sermon taught followers to steer a middle course between self-indulgence and self-denial. The Buddha taught that the way ahead lay in following a life of meditation, morality and wisdom. He taught the Four Noble Truths:

1 That all life contains suffering,
2 That suffering is caused by selfishness
3 That suffering can be avoided by overcoming selfishness
4 That suffering will end if we avoid extremes and follow the Noble Eightfold Path:
- right understanding
- right thought
- right speech
- right conduct
- right occupation
- right effort
- right alertness
- right concentration.

Despite the above, there are no rules as such in Buddhism. Buddhists attempt to make sensible, well-informed choices, knowing that everything they do affects not only themselves but others as well. In order to try to remember to make sensible choices, Buddhists make five promises, or precepts:

1 Not to kill or harm living things
2 Not to take what is not given
3 Not to indulge in sensual pleasures
4 Not to tell lies or say unkind things
5 Not to take drink or drugs which cloud the mind.

Buddhists believe that there have been other Buddhas in history, and that there may be others still to come. They believe that each Bodhisattva goes through many lives, in animal and human births, in preparation for Enlightenment and the state of Nirvana (the ultimate state of perfect peace and joy). The stories of these many and varied births are called the *Jataka Tales*, and are some of the most popular stories of the Buddhist world. It is from these stories that the fables in this chapter have been adapted.

Buddhists believe that the insight, goodness, and moral and intellectual perfection attained by the Buddha, could not have been acquired in a single lifetime. It is believed that these values were accumulated as a result of the continual effort of generations of successive Bodhisattvas, each of whom inherited the qualities of character of the previous Bodhisattvas.

Orthodox Buddhists believe that the origin of the Jatakas is that the Buddha explained and commented on events happening at the time, by recalling similar events from his previous births. The retelling enabled him to point out a moral. The stories he told are said to have been learned by his followers, who repeated them and gave them sacredness because of their identification with a main character and the Buddha himself. The tales, previously merely fables, were now sanctified stories and renamed Jatakas to distinguish them from other fables.

The stories were handed down in the Pali language in which they were composed – this was the common language of the people at the time. There are between 500 and 600 birth stories in total; the exact number is difficult to establish because of repetition, but it is said to be the oldest, most complete and most important collection of folk-lore in existence.

The robbers and the treasure   *Greed*
adapted from the Vedabbha-Jataka

There was once a man in a certain village who knew a magic charm.

If he said the magic words at exactly the right moment in time – when the sun and moon and stars and planets were in particular positions – he could make the sky rain treasure! He could make the sky rain diamonds and emeralds, rubies and sapphires, topaz, aquamarine, silver, gold, garnets, amethyst and pearls.

One day, when the special star time was almost there, the man was caught by robbers.

'Give us money, or we'll kill you!' they said.

'I have no money,' pleaded the man. 'Please let me go. Please don't kill me.'

'Money!' menaced the robbers, and they held a sharp shining knife to his neck.

'I have no money,' said the man again. 'But the special star time's nearly here. I can bring you treasure from the sky. I know the magic words. Look!' And he pointed to the sun which was almost in the highest part of the sky.

As the robbers looked, the man began to recite the words of the magic charm. Suddenly, as if the shimmering sun had broken into a thousand pieces, an explosion of glittering jewels burst from the sky. Their colours were so bright, so brilliant, so dazzling, that the robbers had to hide their eyes from the glare. But as soon as the jewels touched the ground, the robbers scrambled to stuff them into their sacks.

No sooner were their sacks full, and the thieves were deciding what to do with the man, than a second band of robbers appeared. They surrounded the first group and demanded the jewels. 'Give them to us.'

'You don't need these,' said the leader of the first robbers. 'There's plenty more for you. This fellow's a magician. He knows a magic spell. He'll make some more treasure for you then we'll all have some.'

'Go on then,' said the leader of the second robbers. 'Make some treasure for us.'

But the man with the magic charm knew that the special star time had passed. He knew it would be many months, if not years, before the sun and moon and stars and planets would be in exactly the right positions again. He knew there would be no more treasure rain that day, and he told the robbers so.

Their anger was unbelievable. They shouted and swore and shook their fists.

And then the fight broke out.

The man with the magic charm took the opportunity to creep away and hide until it was all over.

The robbers fought so fiercely that soon every one of them was dead except the two leaders.

'Let's not fight any more,' said one. But he thought to himself 'I'll kill him by a different way instead.'

'No, let's not fight,' agreed the other. But he thought to himself 'I'll get rid of him, then all the treasure will be mine.'

Between them they carried the sacks of jewels to a cave, then sat down to decide what to do next.

'I'm hungry,' said one.

'I am too,' said the other. 'I know, let's go and find something to eat.'

'But we can't leave the treasure,' said the first.

'Then one of us can guard the treasure, and one of us can go to find something to eat,' said the other.

And that's exactly what they did. But all the time, they were plotting and planning a way to kill each other.

The robber who was standing guard over the jewels, polished his sword and tested the sharpness of its blade against his finger. 'I'll chop off his head,' he thought.

The robber who was finding food took a small packet of poison out of his pocket. 'I'll poison him,' he thought.

They met again back at the cave, but had no time to talk, because the guard robber flashed his sword in the air, and chopped off the head of the other robber.

'Good!' he said to himself. 'That's the end of him! Now I'm going to sit down and enjoy this food and then I'll start to move this treasure back to my place.'

He sat down and ate the food, but of course he never moved the treasure anywhere, and it stayed in the cave for ever.

cf. 'The Pardoner's Tale' by Chaucer. In this tale, three rioters find a pile of florins. Greed leads them to attempt to trick each other, one is killed by the sword, the other two drink poisoned wine.

The Judas Tree*   *Jumping to conclusions*
adapted from the Kimsukopama-Jataka

There was once a wise king called Brahmadatta, the King of Benares. He had four sons and was concerned about them ruling his kingdom after he had died.

'They're good sons, but sometimes not very bright!' he thought. 'I wonder which of them will be the wisest after I'm gone. I wonder which will make the best king? I wonder how I can find out?'

After a great deal of thought and pondering, the King decided to set them a task; then he would know which son was the wisest – which son could use his brain and think. He called his sons to him.

'I want to know what a Judas Tree looks like,' he said. 'I want you each to find out and report back to let me know. I'm not in a hurry for an answer. It's winter time now, so any time before next winter will do,' and the king swept out of the room.

'A Judas Tree!' said the sons. 'What does he want to know that for?'

'Well, we'd better go and find out,' said the first son, and he set off straight away to search the kingdom for a Judas Tree. It wasn't easy to find one, but eventually a man showed him one near his garden.

'It's not much to look at, is it,' said the first son, as he gazed at the bare brown trunk and the bare brown branches of the Judas Tree. 'It looks dead to me.'

'Well it's winter,' said the man, 'What do you expect?'

The second son eventually got around to finding a Judas Tree in the spring. He saw soft green leaves fluttering from the tree's branches and thought it looked very pretty, but he couldn't imagine why his father had wanted him to find out what it looked like. It looked like any other tree in spring.

The third son found the Judas Tree in the summer. He had almost forgotten what the king had asked him to do, and it was only when he heard some people arranging to meet each other under the shade of the Judas Tree, that he remembered. He had never seen anything as beautiful. The tree's trunk and branches were covered with brilliant pink clusters of flowers, like painted cauliflowers. It was an amazing sight.

'No wonder our Dad asked us to look at this,' he said to himself. 'It's the most beautiful tree in the world.'

The fourth son found a Judas Tree in autumn, but quite by accident. He'd forgotten all about the King asking his sons to find the tree and tell him what it looked like. He was searching for conkers with his friends, when suddenly one of them said 'Oh look. A Judas Tree. Let's pick some of its fruit.' The King's son looked at the tree and saw the trunk and branches laden with clusters of fruits. But the fruits were not as interesting as conkers. He didn't think they would be able to play games with the Judas Tree fruits, like they did with the horse chestnut fruits, but they picked some all the same.

A little while later, the King called his four sons to his side again.

'Well?' he asked. 'Have you done what I asked you to do? Have you found a Judas Tree and can you describe it to me?'

'Yes!' said the sons all together.

'It's boring and brown and dead-looking,' said the first.

'No it's not,' said the third. 'It's amazingly beautiful and the brightest pink I've ever seen.'

'Rubbish!' said the second. 'You must be colour blind if you think it's pink. It's light green.'

'It's not,' said the fourth. 'It's brown. But it's not dull and dead-looking, it's covered in fruits.'

'It's a brown stumpy thing.'

'It's brilliant pink!'

'It's green!'

'It's knobbly brown!'

'No it's not!'

'Yes it is!'

'No it's not!'

The argument grew more heated as the sons shouted and argued with each other.

'Stop!' roared the King.

'You are all even more foolish that I thought you were. You stupid boys! You can none of you see past the end of your nose. You have all seen the Judas Tree, but you have all bothered to look at it only once. None of you has asked what the tree might look like at a different time. Not one of you has listened to the views of the others. You are all so sure that you are right you have closed you ears to everyone else's ideas. You won't understand anything unless you look at it in different ways and at different times. Not one of you is fit to be the king after me.'

And King Brahmadatta felt very sad that his sons had used their eyes but not their brains.

* *The Judas Tree of the title is the genus Cercis. The trees are found in Eastern Asia, are deciduous, and have cauliflorous flowers borne directly on the trunk. Further information and illustration can be found in The Oxford Encyclopaedia of Trees of the World, published by the Oxford University Press.*

cf. *'The blind men and the elephant', found in Buddhist literature. Several blind men are sent to examine an elephant. Each man describes the animal differently, and each is convinced he is right. The moral is drawn that nothing is properly understood unless it is looked at from a variety of angles.*

The hare's self-sacrifice   *Generosity*
adapted from the Sasa-Jataka

There was once a wise young hare who lived in a wood with his three friends – the otter, the jackal and the monkey. The four animals hunted by themselves each day, but each evening they met together for their evening meal, they talked together as friends do, and the hare, being the wisest, tried to teach the others the right way to live.

One day the hare said to his friends 'Tomorrow is a fasting day. We must eat nothing, but we must also try to be kind to any beggars we see, by giving them something to eat. Can you do that?'

The three friends said they would try.

The next day each of the four of them set off as usual to go hunting. The otter found seven fine fish buried in the sand of the riverbed, and took them home. The jackal found a pot of milk left behind by a shepherd, and the monkey found a bunch of mangoes growing high in a tree. They took the milk and the mangoes home. The hare found nothing except some grass, which he gathered in a bunch.

'This isn't going to make much of a meal for anyone,' he said to himself. 'I can't offer this to a beggar if I meet one. But I can offer myself. If I meet a beggar I shall give him my body to eat.'

Now it just so happened that Sakka – the greatest of the gods – had heard the hare's thoughts and decided to put him to the test. Sakka turned himself into a beggar and went to the home of the four friends.

He asked the otter for food.

'Yes, of course,' said the otter. 'I have seven fine fish here. You're more than welcome to have them. Here,' and he held out the fish to the beggar.

'Thank you,' said the man. 'I'll come back for them later.'

Then he asked the jackal for food.

'Yes,' said the jackal. 'I have a pot of milk here. You can have it with pleasure.'

'Thank you,' said the beggar. 'I'll come back for it later.'

The man then spoke to the monkey.

'I have some mangoes,' said the monkey. 'You can have them.'

'Thank you,' said Sakka. 'I'll come back for them later.'

Then Sakka, in his beggar disguise, turned to the hare.

'I have nothing for you to eat,' said the hare. 'But you can eat me. I know you cannot kill me, for that's against the law, but if you build a fire and give me a shout when it's blazing nicely, I'll jump in it and you can eat my roasted meat when I'm cooked.'

'Thank you,' said Sakka, and he magically made a fire appear in front of them.

The hare walked up to the fire, then shook his coat so that any tiny insects who happened to be caught in his fur would not die with him. Then he walked into the fire and lay down.

But the hare did not burn. The flames felt icy cold instead of roasting hot.

'What's happening?' said the hare. 'Why am I still alive?'

'Because you tried to give me everything you had,' said the man. 'You were prepared to give me your life. There is no greater gift than that.' And Sakka lifted the hare out of the fire, and set him down on the grass, perfectly unharmed.

'I am Sakka', he went on, 'and I shall reward your generosity so that everyone shall know of your kindness.'

Sakka pointed his finger and drew the sign of the hare on the face of the moon, so that everyone would remember the generous hare. Then he went back to his place in heaven, and the four friends continued to live happily together in the wood.

NB. This story is believed not to have a parallel outside Buddhist sources.

The woodpecker, the tortoise and the antelope   *Loyalty*
adapted from the Kurungamiga-Jataka

Once upon a time when the Bodhisattva came to this earth as an antelope, he lived in a forest near a lake. Nearby lived a tortoise and a woodpecker, and all three were the best of friends. They liked to talk together, and eat together; make plans together and play together. They got along very well together and knew they would be friends always.

One day a hunter came to that part of the forest and noticed the antelope's footprints leading down to the water's edge.

'I'll have him!' thought the hunter. 'He'll make a good meal or two with meat to spare.'

The hunter set a trap, well hidden in the bushes and reeds by the very edge of the lake. The antelope, suspecting nothing, came down to the water's edge as usual to drink. He was always cautious and careful, listening for any sound, any danger; but he heard nothing. He drank from the cool clean crystal clear water and turned to go back to his friends.

Then snap! The hard cruel metal trap caught his leg in its fierce jaws. The antelope cried out in pain and fell to the ground. The more he moved, the more the metal teeth of the trap bit into his flesh. Yet not to move was unthinkable. He had to get free of the trap.

The woodpecker and the tortoise had heard the savage crack of the trap closing and had heard the cry of the antelope. Their instinct was to run – to save themselves, to get away from whatever danger was in the forest. But their loyalty to their friend made them hesitate. They couldn't leave him caught in the trap. They knew what would happen; he would be unable to free himself from the trap's grip and would become weaker and weaker in the struggle, eventually to die slowly and in pain. No, they couldn't leave him to that.

'But what can we do?' said the tortoise. 'We are no match against the skills of the hunter.'

'There are two of us and only one of him,' said the woodpecker. 'Here's what we'll do,' and he told the tortoise his plan.

The tortoise hurried to the antelope and began to bite and gnaw through the leather straps which held together the metal jaws of the trap. All the time she was aware that the hunter might come at any minute, and that she wouldn't be able to escape quickly. She, too, could be caught.

Meanwhile the woodpecker waited for the hunter to come along the path. Soon he appeared, and the woodpecker flew at his face. The hunter grabbed at the woodpecker... and missed. The woodpecker flew at him again, and again and again. Each time, the hunter grabbed at the flapping bird... but each time he missed. The woodpecker knew that he risked getting caught by the hunter, but he also knew that the longer he distracted the man in this way, the longer the tortoise would have to try and bite through the leather straps of the trap.

The tortoise by now was in great difficulty. His mouth was sore and bleeding and his teeth were worn down. But still he kept biting the leather. At last the straps gave way, the trap opened and the antelope struggled to its feet.

'Run,' shouted the tortoise. 'He's coming.' And sure enough, the hunter was running along the path towards the trap. He was taking no notice now of the flapping woodpecker.

'So!' thundered the hunter. 'Escaped have you? Well if I can't have one of you I'll have the other,' and he grabbed hold of the tortoise and stuffed him into a sack.

Now it was the turn of the antelope to try to save his friend. He ran in front of the man, pretending to be hurt. The man, thinking he would catch the antelope again, dropped the sack and followed him. The antelope led the hunter deeper and deeper into the forest, along twisting turning tracks that the hunter had never seen before. Even though his leg hurt, the antelope ran on, always a little ahead of the hunter, always leading him deeper into the dark forest.

Then, quite suddenly, the antelope changed direction. He disappeared under the bushes and doubled back the way he had come, leaving the hunter standing alone, stranded and lost. The antelope kept on running until he found the sack with the tortoise in it. The woodpecker was already trying to untie the neck of the sack to let the tortoise free.

'Well!' said the tortoise. 'That was a near thing. Thank you for coming to my rescue.'

'Thank you for coming to mine,' said the antelope. 'That's what friends are for,' said the woodpecker, and they all agreed.

Then they helped each other home, and all lived happily ever after.

cf. 'The travellers and the bear', page 154. The theme of loyalty is treated differently by Aesop, as he describes the actions of a disloyal friend.

See also 'The pigeon and the ant' on page 155, in which animals repay each other's loyalty.

The stolen jewels
adapted from the Mahasara-Jataka

Jumping to conclusions

There was once a monkey who climbed to the top of the tallest tree in the royal palace gardens. He liked it there. He could see almost everything from there. He could see the guards in their sentry boxes at the palace gates, he could see the rest of the monkeys playing in the gardens, he could see a man walking in the woods next to the gardens, and he could see the queen by the lake with her servant girl.

He watched the queen as she started to swim in the lake. She was a good swimmer. He watched the servant girl as she folded up the queen's clothes and put them in a tidy pile on the grass. He watched as she put the queen's jewels on top of the pile, and he watched as the servant girl sat down on the grass and fell asleep.

The monkey slowly climbed down the tree and crept towards the queen's clothes. He checked that the girl was still asleep and that the queen had not seen him, then he carefully stretched out his paw and stole the queen's beautiful pearl necklace. Then, quick as as flash, he ran, back to the tree, up to the top, where nobody could find him.

The servant girl woke up. She saw that the queen was still swimming and she glanced at the pile of royal clothes.

Gone!

The pearl necklace from the top of the pile was gone! It had been stolen!

'Help,' she shouted. 'Guards, help! The queen's jewels have been stolen. Catch the thief!'

The guards ran to search the grounds. The thief couldn't be far away.

No-one in the gardens, no-one by the lake, no-one in the greenhouse, no-one by the stream; but there, look, there's a man walking in the woods. 'He's here!' shouted the guards. 'This man is the thief! Catch him!'

The man, who of course had nothing to do with the jewels, heard the guards running after him, and took to his heels as fast as he could. But the guards were too many, too fast, too strong. They caught the man and began to beat him.

'Where is the necklace?' they demanded. 'What have you done with it?'

The man was so afraid of the guards and of the beating he was getting, he said the first thing that came into his head.

'I gave it to the cook. Now please let me go.'

The guards threw him to the ground and went to find the cook.

'Where is it?' they shouted. 'Where have you put it?'

The cook felt so afraid, she said the first thing she thought of.

'I gave it to the gardener.'

The guards went to find the gardener.

'We know you've stolen the queen's necklace,' they shouted. 'Give it to us.'

The gardener had never felt so frightened. He would say anything just to get rid of the guards.

'I haven't got it... I gave it to a boy... a boy in the kitchen... it wasn't me.'

The guards went to find the boy.

'Where's the queen's necklace?' they said.

'I don't know what you're talking about,' said the boy. 'I've never even seen it. It's nothing to do with me.'

Just then, a wise man came walking by.

'What's going on?' he asked.

The guards told him.

'I don't think it has anything to do with any of these people,' said the wise man. 'After all, the necklace was stolen from inside the gardens, and none of these people were there at the time.'

'But no-one was there at the time,' said the guards.

'No,' said the wise man. 'No-one, except the monkeys. Leave it to me.'

The wise man hurried off to the market, and came back with lots of strings of brightly coloured beads. He took the beads into the royal gardens and began to hang them from the branches of all the trees. No sooner were the beads in the trees, than the monkeys came. They snatched the beads and dangled them from their arms and legs. They wound them round their heads and looped them on their tails. They danced and chattered and happily played.

But one of the monkeys felt angry.

'It's not fair,' he cried. 'I was the only one with beads, and now you've all got them. Anyway, I don't care, my beads are better than yours! My beads are beautiful. My beads are shinier. My beads are *real!*' And he flourished the queen's pearl necklace under their noses.

There was silence in the royal garden.

Then the wise man spoke. 'I thought that would work,' he said. He turned to the guards, 'Perhaps in future you should be sure of your facts before you accuse people of theft.'

And then he turned to the monkeys, 'You can keep your beads,' he said. 'But you,' and he pointed to the monkey who had stolen the queen's necklace, 'You can give the pearl necklace to me, and you can go without beads!'

The grateful parrot   *Loyalty*
adapted from the Mahasuka-Jataka

There was once a huge flock of parrots who lived in a forest of fig trees by the side of a river. The parrots had lived there for some considerable time, and all had gone well, until one day the king of the parrots noticed that the trees were not as healthy as they had been.

The leaves were not as bright, the figs were not as juicy and tender, the tree trunks were not quite as firm and sturdy as before.

'Something's wrong,' said the king of the parrots.

At first he said nothing to the other parrots, so as not to alarm them. But soon they noticed for themselves.

'What are we going to do?' they asked their king. 'If the trees die we'll have nowhere to live. If the trees die we'll have nothing to eat. If the trees die, then we'll die too. What are we going to do?'

'These trees have been good friends to us,' said the king. 'They have given us food and shelter all these years. We can't leave them now.'

'But they're dying!' said the parrots. 'And if we stay here, we'll die too. We're off to find somewhere else to live.' And with that, all the parrots flew away to find another forest to live in.

All, that is, except one. The king of the parrots couldn't go. He'd lived in his tree so long, he simply couldn't bear to leave it.

'You are my friend,' he said to the tree. 'You and I have been together for a long time. I'll not leave you.'

Now it just so happened that Sakka – the greatest of the gods – had heard this, and he decided to put the parrot king to the test, to see how faithful he really was.

Sakka made the fig tree shrivel and wither and lose all its leaves. But the parrot king stayed with the tree.

Sakka made the tree lose all its figs so that the king had nothing to eat. But the parrot king stayed with his tree.

Sakka made the tree trunk full of holes, he made dust of its wood, and he sent a fierce wind to buffet and blow the tree. But the parrot king clung on to the dead branches and closed his eyes against the dust, and stayed with his tree.

Sakka then turned himself into a goose and went to see the parrot king.

'All the rest of the parrots have flown away to a new home,' he said. 'Why don't you go too?'

'This tree has been a good friend to me,' said the parrot king. 'I'm not going to leave it now that it's ill and dying. I shall stay with it as long as it needs me.'

'You are a loyal and faithful friend,' said Sakka. 'If I were to grant you a wish, what would you have?'

'I would like this tree to live again,' said the parrot king. 'I would like it to have green leaves, and a fine fat trunk. I would like it to have ripe juicy figs once more.'

Sakka said not a word but became himself again instead of the goose, and walked to the edge of the river. He scooped up a handful of water, and hurried back to the fig tree. Sakka sprinkled the water on the tree and immediately it grew tall and straight and green again. It grew leaves and flowers and the sweetest figs in the space of a second.

'There!' said Sakka. 'A fine fat healthy fig tree for a true and loyal friend.'

'Thank you,' said the king of the parrots.

'Thank you,' said Sakka, 'for being faithful.'

The jackal's spell   *Dishonesty*
adapted from the Sabbadatha-Jataka

There was once a wise man who knew the secret of making all things on earth quiet... and calm... and still... and peaceful... and obedient. He could do this by saying some magic words. As soon as a man, or an insect, or an animal, or a bird heard the words, it would become very tranquil... very serene... very restful... and very relaxed.

One day the wise man went into the forest to recite the words, and to practise them. But whilst he was doing this, a jackal overheard him. The jackal listened to the magic words very carefully, and soon knew them well enough to remember them.

'I'm going to try this out,' said the jackal to himself, and he ran off to find some animals on which to try out the magic words.

First he spoke the words to a cat, then a dog, then a mouse and a hedgehog, a horse and a rabbit. Then he tried out the words on a bird, a spider, a lizard and a frog.

And they worked!

The words worked! They made all the creatures quiet and calm and still.

'With these magic words I could be king,' thought the jackal. 'I could make all the people and animals obey me... I *will* make all the people and animals obey me! I *will* be king!'

The jackal went off to find a lion and an elephant, and said the magic words to them. As soon as they were quiet and calm, the jackal climbed up on to the back of the lion, then ordered the lion to climb up on to the back of the elephant. Then, perched up there on top of them both, he marched into the city and demanded to see the king.

'I am going to be the new king here!' he said to the king. 'So you can move out!'

Now the king didn't quite know what to do about this, so he sent for the wise man.

'Leave this to me,' said the wise man. 'I'll sort him out!' and he turned to speak to the jackal.

'How are you going to take charge of the city?' he asked.

'That's easy,' said the jackal. 'I'm going to tell my lion to roar, then all the people in the city will be frightened, and I can take charge.'

'Mmmm!' said the wise man, and he turned to whisper to the king. 'Go quickly and tell all the people and all the animals to block up their ears,' he said. The king hurried off.

Then the wise man turned to the jackal again.

'And how will you make your lion roar?' he asked. 'It won't roar just because you tell it to!'

'Oh yes it will,' said the jackal. 'Just you wait and see!' The jackal looked down at the sleepy quiet lion beneath him. 'ROAR!' he shouted.

The lion did exactly as it was told, and let out a huge, deafening, mighty, tremendous, ear-splitting ROAR.

Of course, the people and the animals of the city took absolutely no notice at all, because they had all done what the king had asked, and blocked up their ears. So no-one actually heard the roar at all. Except, that is, for the elephant, who was standing quietly, still with the lion and the jackal on his back.

At the sound of the mighty roar, the elephant almost jumped out of his skin. The jackal overbalanced and crashed to the ground with the lion sprawling on top of him, and the elephant trod on them both as he rushed to get out of the way of the dreadful noise and pandemonium.

The wise man came and looked at the sorry-looking jackal. 'I think the people can unblock their ears now,' he said. 'I don't think we'll be troubled again by a jackal wanting to be king. And I think I know a certain jackal who will be careful about stealing other people's words in future! Don't I?'

But the jackal was so ashamed he said... nothing.

The crocodile and the monkey   *Strongest may not be most clever*
adapted from the Sumsumara-Jataka

There was once a crocodile and his wife who lived in a deep, dark, fast-flowing river. One day the female crocodile said 'I just must have a monkey's heart to eat. I'm so hungry. Find me one please.'

'I can't get you a monkey's heart to eat!' said the male crocodile. 'Monkeys live on land and we live in the water, I can't catch a monkey for you. You'll have to eat something else instead.'

'No,' said his wife. 'I shall die if I don't have a monkey's heart to eat. You must find me one.'

The male crocodile knew there was a fine strong healthy monkey who lived by the side of the river, but he also knew that the monkey was brave and clever and sensible. He didn't think he would have any chance at all of catching the monkey, let alone of killing it so that he could give its heart to his wife.

'But please,' said his wife again and again.

'I shall have to trick the monkey,' thought the crocodile. 'It's the only way I'll catch it.'

The crocodile started lying at the edge of the river every day, when he knew the monkey would come to drink. He made sure he spoke to the monkey every day, so that the monkey would get to know him, and not feel afraid. But the monkey never came too near; he always stayed just out of reach. He knew he mustn't get too friendly with the crocodile; he knew that a crocodile could easily eat him, even a monkey as big and strong as he.

One day the crocodile said to him, 'Why do you eat the fruit of these trees here, at this side of the river. Don't you know that the fruit at the other side of the river is better?'

'It doesn't matter if it is,' said the monkey. 'I can't get over there. The river is too deep and dark and fast-flowing for me to cross it.'

'I'll carry you across on my back,' said the crocodile. 'I'll look after you. I won't let you drown,' and he smiled a large wide crocodile smile.

'All right,' said the monkey. 'I'll trust you.'

The crocodile climbed a little way out of the water, and the monkey scrambled onto his back. They started out across the river. The crocodile was a good strong swimmer and the monkey felt safe on his back.

But, half way across the deep dark wide river, the crocodile plunged the monkey under the water.

'Hey! Don't do that,' spluttered the monkey. 'You're drowning me!'

'I'm going to kill you,' said the crocodile. 'You don't think I'm carrying you over the river just to be nice do you? Oh no! I'm going to have your heart. My wife wants to eat it.'

'Well, thank you for telling me!' said the monkey. 'At least I know what you're going to do with me.' But all the time the monkey was talking, he was frantically trying to think of a plan to save himself; a plan to outwit the crocodile; a plan to trick him.

'But you do know that monkeys don't keep their hearts inside their bodies, don't you?' asked the monkey, as an idea came into his head. 'I mean, it's quite obvious if you think about it. If we kept our hearts inside our bodies like everyone else, they'd get knocked to pieces as we swing about in the trees. Oh no, we don't keep our hearts inside us.'

'Then where do you keep them?' said the crocodile.

'Over there,' said the monkey, pointing back to the edge of the river where they'd just come from. 'We keep out hearts hidden in the fruits of those trees over there.'

'Really?' said the crocodile. 'Well, I never knew that!'

'Oh yes,' said the monkey. 'In fact, if you turn round and take me back, I'll show you my heart, hidden in one of those figs on that tree by the rock.'

'Well, that's very kind of you,' said the crocodile, and he turned round and began to swim back the way he had come, anxious to get to the trees quickly so that the monkey could show him his heart, which the crocodile could then steal to take home to his wife.

But when they reached the edge of the river, the monkey jumped off the crocodile's back. 'You silly old croc,' he said. 'Do you really think we keep our hearts in the trees? And if we did, do you really think I'd show you where mine is so that you can steal it? You might be big and strong and fierce and scary, but you've got no sense,' and with that the monkey disappeared into the trees and the crocodile never saw him again.

cf. 'The sea monster and the fox', page 98. In this Jewish version of the story, a fox outwits a fish who is acting on behalf of the sea monster. By claiming he has left his heart on land, the fox persuades the fish to swim back to shore. A story 'The ape and the crocodile', virtually identical to this Buddhist version, is found in the Hindu Panchatantra. *The Hindu story is longer than the above, and is presented as a frame story for an inner tale, 'The ass without heart and ears,'*

The jackal and the crow
adapted from the Jambukhadaka-Jataka

Once, there was a most beautiful orchard of rose-apple trees, and in one of the trees lived a wise tree spirit. No-one could see him, but he could see and hear everything and everyone in the orchard.

One day he saw a crow fly to the topmost branch of one of the trees. She started to eat the apples on the highest branches, and the tree spirit knew that they were the sweetest, the juiciest, the best apples in the orchard.

Someone else had seen the crow land in the tree and start eating. A jackal who came to the orchard every day hunting and scavenging for food, had seen her.

'That crow is eating the best apples,' thought the jackal. 'She's eating the best apples on those high branches that I can't reach. It isn't fair! I come here every day and I've never managed to have any of the best fruit. I'm going to get her to give me some.'

'Throw me some apples down,' called the jackal. But the crow merely cawed loudly and carried on eating.

'I said give me some fruit,' shouted the jackal. But again, the crow just cawed at him and carried on eating.

'I want some of those apples,' yelled the jackal.

'Caw, caw-caw, cauauauw!' said the crow.

'What a dreadful din she makes,' said the jackal to himself, but the noise gave him an idea. 'If I flatter her, and tell her she's beautiful; if I lie and tell her what a wonderful voice she has, she may share the fruit with me,'

'Hello,' called the jackal in his softest voice. 'I'm so glad you've come to my orchard.'

'Caw?' said the crow.

'Yes, I'm so pleased,' said the jackal. 'It's wonderful to hear such sweet singing. We don't usually hear such melodious music in these parts. You really must be so proud of your splendid voice.'

'Caw?' said the crow again.

'And your beauty,' went on the jackal, 'Your beauty is so marvellous to behold. Your feathers glisten like polished ebony, and your beak is perfection itself. Why, even the peacock pales to nothing next to your splendour!'

The crow stopped eating her apples and looked down at the jackal. 'What an ugly fellow,' she thought, 'But if I tell him he is handsome, it might be worth my while.'

'Well thank you for your kind words,' she said in her sweetest voice. 'I am so pleased to come here into your orchard and meet such a handsome, strong, noble animal as yourself. I cannot ever remember seeing anyone so good-looking, so elegant, so graceful, so princely. The others in this orchard are so lucky to have someone like you who can teach them to appreciate beauty and music. Oh yes, you are indeed the most wonderful jackal.' And she shook the rose-apple tree, so that some of the fruit would fall down to the jackal below.

The wise tree spirit had, of course, been watching all the false flattery, and listening to all the lies. 'I can't stand this,' he suddenly said. 'They are two prize liars together. It's time I got rid of them both!'

And with that, the wise tree spirit turned himself into a monster and frightened them both away. The rose apple orchard returned to normal, and the crow and the jackal were never seen again.

cf. Aesop's 'The fox and the crow' in which the fox flatters the crow in order to make her drop some food. She succumbs to the insincere flattery and loses a piece of cheese to the fox.

The jackal in Indian fable takes the place of the Aesopian fox to portray a sly, artful, cunning, wily, crafty character.

The foolish crow

Pride/envy

adapted from the Viraka-Jataka

There was once a beautiful sea-bird who lived in a rocky bay of the coastline. The other birds called him The Strong One because of his skills at fishing and diving. He would fly out over the bay, and hover high above the waves... watching... waiting... Then, when he saw a fish, deep beneath the surface of the sea, he would push his wings behind him in a wide vee-shape, and dive like a dart, straight into the sea without making a ripple or a splash. He always caught his fish.

One day, a crow from the city came, quite by accident, to the cliffs by the sea-bird's bay. He watched the sea-bird. He saw how he fished. He noticed how skilful he was.

'He can fish really well,' said the crow to himself. 'If I was to stay here instead of going home to the city, I could be his servant, I could help him, and then he would feed me and I would never go hungry.'

The crow waited until the sea-bird returned to the cliff face.

'I've watched you fish,' said the crow. 'You do it really well. I'm so impressed by your skills that I'd like to stay here and be your servant, instead of going back to the city. Will you let me? I could help you with anything you want me to do.'

'That's very kind of you,' said the sea-bird. 'It would be useful to have someone to help me. I know you are not able to fish, but you can help me with other things, and in return I will feed you with as much fish as you can eat.'

'It's a deal then,' said the crow.

'It's a deal,' answered the sea-bird.

And so the crow began work as the sea-bird's servant, and the sea-bird made sure the crow never went hungry. For a while all went well. Then the crow began to have second thoughts about the arrangement.

'It's all very well,' he said to himself. 'But I don't much like being a servant. I can never please myself; I always have to do what he wants me to do. I can never do what *I* want to do. I'm fed up with this job. I think I'm going to leave.'

But then the crow remembered his life in the city, and remembered how hard it was to find food each day. He thought of all the fish he was able to eat, now that he lived near the sea.

'No!' he said. 'I won't leave! But I'll catch my own fish in future. I don't need *him* anymore. I'm just as good as him, if not better. I've watched him fish and I know what to do. I'll do it myself from now on.' And the crow went to tell the sea-bird that he was leaving his job, and in future would do his own fishing thank you!

'But you can't,' said the sea-bird. 'You're not a sea-bird. If you try to fish like we do, you'll kill yourself. You'll be dashed to pieces in the waves. You'll drown. You don't belong to the sea-bird family. You're a land bird.'

'You can't tell me what to do any more,' shouted the crow.

'I'm not trying to tell you what to do,' said the sea-bird. 'I'm trying to make you see sense.'

'You think you're better than me,' said the crow, 'but I'm just as good as you.'

'I don't think I'm better than you,' said the sea-bird. 'I'm just different that's all. I'm a water bird and you're a land bird.'

'I'm not! I'm a sea bird,' said the crow, and he swooped from the cliff face and flew out over the sea. He hovered for a second, then dived down in a flurry of black feathers. He disappeared beneath the swirling waves... and was never seen again.

cf. La Fontaine's 'Crow and the peacock feathers'. In this parallel story a crow wants to become a peacock. He adorns himself with peacocks' tail feathers and struts about, only to be pecked almost to death by their owners. He tries to return to his flock, but is killed by them since they don't recognise him.

See also 'The crow and the swan' page 151, The same theme is also explored in La Fontaine's 'Crow and the eagle', and Aesop's 'The donkey and the dog', in which animals envy each other to the extent of wanting to become the other creature, with disastrous results.

Further reading

For teachers
A Short History of Buddhism Edward Conze (Allen and Unwin 1980)
Buddhism in the Twentieth Century Peggy Morgan (Hutton 1985)
Buddhism; Its Essence and Development Edward Conze (Harper & Cassirer 1975)
Buddhist Scriptures Edward Conze (Penguin Classics 1969)

Six Religions in the Twentieth Century W.Owen Cole with Peggy Morgan (Hulton Educational 1984)
The Life of the Buddha H. Saddhatissa (Unwin Paperbacks 1976)
The World of Buddhism Heinz Bechert and Richard Gombrich (Thames and Hudson 1984)
What the Buddha Taught Walpola Sri Rahula (Gordon Fraser 1982 reprint)

For children
I am a Buddhist 'My Belief' Series (Franklin Watts 1986)
Our Culture – Buddhist 'Our Culture' Series (Franklin Watts 1988)
Ten Buddhist Fables John Snelling (Buddhist Publishing Group 1984)
The Buddhist World Anne Bancroft (MacDonald 1984)
The Life of the Buddha John Snelling (Wayland 1987)
The Story of the Buddha Association of Buddhist Women UK (London Buddhist Vihara)

Useful addresses

Books from India, 45 Museum Street, London WC1
Buddhist Publishing Group, Box 136, Leicester LE2 1DZ.
Friends of the Western Buddhist Order, The London Buddhist Centre, 51 Roman Road, Bethnal Green, London E2.
The Buddhist Society, 58 Ecclestone Square, London SW1V 1PH.

Christianity

Christianity is the fourth oldest of the six major world religions, and is the world's largest religion. It has an estimated following of 1500 million people, and today Christians are found in almost every country. There are four major branches of Christianity – Orthodox, Roman Catholic, Protestant and Pentecostal, and some 22,000 different Christian groups. Central to all branches of Christianity, however, is the belief in Jesus of Nazareth.

Christianity, in common with the other five major world religions, began in Asia, despite the popular thinking that Christianity and Judaism are western, and Buddhism, Hinduism, Islam and Sikhism eastern. Christianity stems from Judaism, since Jesus himself was a Jew.

The birth of Jesus of Nazareth, between the 7th and 5th centuries BCE, marks the beginning of Christianity. At the age of 30, Jesus was baptized by John the Baptist, a prophet who heralded the coming of one greater than himself. Jesus then gathered around him the twelve disciples (apostles), and during the next three years he preached, taught and healed the sick.

At the age of 33 Jesus was arrested and put to death by crucifixion, a common method of execution at the time. Christians believe that Jesus rose from the dead three days later, and appeared to his friends and disciples on several occasions during the next 40 days. He then returned to his Father – God – in heaven.

During the 200 years after Jesus' ministry, Christianity spread to India, Africa and Europe. It is uncertain how and when the religion reached Britain, but it would seem likely to have been brought by traders and merchants. The first Christian martyrs in Britain are named as Aaron, Alban and Julian. They are thought to have lived and died between 200 and 300 CE.

Christians believe in one God who is omnipresent and the creator of all that there is. They believe that Jesus is the Son of God who died to save mankind, but that he rose from the dead and is 'alive' today. Christians believe that Jesus was Son of God and Son of Man, divine and human. They believe in the Holy Trinity – God the Father, God the Son, and God the Spirit. Through the Holy

Spirit Christians believe that God is alive in the hearts of each of them. Christians believe that they will have life after death through Jesus Christ.

The essence of Christian belief is expressed in the creeds. The Apostles' Creed, which follows, is used in the western church, whilst the longer Nicene Creed is used world-wide. The Athanasian Creed is complex and little used in church services. The creeds are statements of belief.

The Apostles' Creed
   I believe in God, the Father Almighty,
   Maker of heaven and earth:
   And in Jesus Christ his only son our Lord,
   Who was conceived by the Holy Ghost,
   Born of the Virgin Mary,
   Suffered under Pontius Pilate,
   Was crucified, dead, and buried,
   He descended into hell;
   The third day he rose again from the dead,
   He ascended into heaven
   And sitteth on the right hand of God the Father Almighty;
   From thence he shall come to judge the quick and the dead.
   I believe in the Holy Ghost;
   The Holy Catholic Church;
   The Communion of Saints;
   The Forgiveness of sins;
   The Resurrection of the body;
   And the Life everlasting. Amen.

Christians try to live their lives according to the teaching of Christ. In Matthew 22:34-40, a teacher of the Law tries to trap Jesus by asking the question 'Which is the greatest commandment in the Law?'

Jesus answered " 'Love the Lord your God with all your heart, with all your soul, and with all your mind.' This is the greatest and most important commandment. The second most important commandment is like it: 'Love your neighbour as you love yourself.' The whole Law of Moses and the teachings of the prophets depend on these two commandments."

The stories in this section of *Share Our World* have been adapted from folk stories, many of which were devised by Christian priests. The giants, monsters, fiends, devils and dragons represent evil which must be overcome by good. Yet on another level, according to the devout Christian missionaries, the giants and dragons of these tales personify the old religions, and the stories themselves allegorize the struggle between the new religion of Christianity and the old religions. Other stories were invented tales to account for phenomena beyond the people's comprehension.

The Pedlar of Swaffham   *What you look for may be under your nose*
adapted from English folk-lore

There was once a pedlar, called John, who lived in Swaffham in Norfolk. He lived with his wife and family in a small house. He was hard-working and honest and good, but very poor, and each day it became more and more difficult to manage on what little money they had.

'I don't know what we're going to do,' said John one day.

'Something will turn up,' said his wife.

That night, John had a dream. He dreamed he had to go to London Bridge, and wait there for someone to tell him some good news; some news so wonderful that all his worries would disappear.

In the morning, John told his wife about the dream, but she laughed and told him to take no notice of it. John tried to forget the strange dream, but somehow it wouldn't go out of his head.

That night, and the next night, John had the same dream again, and on the third day he had made a decision.

'I'm going to London,' he told his wife. 'I am going to stand on London Bridge to see if I hear some good news.'

'But you can't go all that way!' she said. 'And you haven't got money to squander and waste in silly trips to London. You stay at home and concentrate on working.'

'No,' said John. 'This is something I have to do. I must go and stand on London Bridge and see if the dream is true.'

'It's a waste of time and money,' said his wife, but nothing she could say or do would make John change his mind.

He set off for London.

He had no money for a carriage, so he walked. Four days it took him. He had no money for a bed at night. He slept by hedgerows or ditches, haystacks or walls. At last he arrived in London. John had never been there before, but he had no difficulty in finding London Bridge, everyone knew where it was.

In those days, the bridge had houses and shops along it, and it was a busy, bustling, congested place. John stood at one end of the bridge... and waited. He waited all day. But no-one spoke to him. No-one took any notice of him. No-one gave him any news of any kind. That night John curled up to sleep, hungry and cold, against the wall of someone's house.

'Perhaps I'll stand at the other end of the bridge today,' he said to himself the next morning. 'Perhaps I'll hear the good news at that end.' So John walked to the other end of London Bridge and waited... all day. But no-one talked to him.

No-one came near him. No-one gave him any news at all. That night John spent a few pence on a bowl of soup and a loaf of bread from one of the shops, and he slept, uncomfortably, against the wall of the bridge.

'Today I'll stand in the middle of the bridge,' he said to himself the next morning. Perhaps today I'll hear the good news I've been waiting for.' John took up a position in the middle of the bridge... and waited... all day. Nothing. No-one. No news. No information.

That night he was unhappier than he had ever been before. 'Tomorrow I'll go home,' he said to himself. 'I was wrong to come. It was a silly idea, a silly dream. I'll go home first thing in the morning.' That night John slept in the doorway of a butcher's shop, to try to keep out of the rain.

In the morning, the owner of the shop woke him up.

'What you doing in my shop doorway,' he snarled. 'Get away. Haven't you got a home to go to?'

'I'm going home today,' said John. 'I've been waiting for some news, that's why I've been here,' and he told the butcher all about his dream and his journey to London.

The butcher had never heard anything so funny in all his life. 'Oh ho, I'll keep my customers amused with this story for weeks. I wouldn't believe anyone could be so stupid as to follow a dream. I mean, I've had a dream too, but I'm not going all the way to Swaffham to see it it's true,' and the butcher burst out laughing all over again.

'Swaffham, you say?' said John.

'Yes. Never heard of the place,' said the butcher. 'But I had this dream about a tree in a pedlar's garden. I dreamed that there was treasure hidden under it. But I'm certainly not travelling to Swaffham to see if it's true.'

The butcher was still laughing heartily as John turned away and began the long journey home to Swaffham. Four long days it took, and all the time John thought of the big oak tree at the bottom of his garden. Could it be true? Could it really be true that there was treasure buried in his own garden, and that he had travelled all the way to London to hear of it?

As soon as he arrived home he grabbed a spade, and, much to the astonishment of his wife dug and dug under the oak tree. Nothing. He called to his wife to help. Nothing. He asked his children to join in the search. Nothing.

Then his spade hit something hard and metallic. A chest. An old chest made of iron. They hauled it up out of the ground. They opened it. Gold and silver coins, precious jewels and ornaments of bronze spilled out onto the soil.

'Just fancy!' said John's wife. 'It was here in our own garden all the time. And you had to go all the way to London to hear about it.'

John and his wife gave some of the treasure to the church which needed repairing. Then they bought a new house, and lived very comfortably for the rest of their lives.

Saint Ulric and the greedy boy

Greed/selfishness

adapted from a Somerset folk legend

There was once a boy called Dick who was one of twelve children. He had a mother, but no father, for he had died some years before. The family had not much money and it was difficult to feed so many children, but the neighbours were kind and used to help out by sometimes giving Dick's mother a sack of potatoes or a bag of flour, a few vegetables, a dozen eggs, or even a chicken occasionally.

There was however a problem. Dick was greedy. He liked to have his share of the food, but he also liked to have his brothers' and sisters' share too. No matter how often his mother told him that it wasn't fair to eat more than them, he took no notice and continued to be greedy.

If Dick was given something to eat when he was out, he would gobble it all up before he got home. It wouldn't occur to him to save it and share it with the others. If Dick woke up in the middle of the night and felt hungry, he would creep downstairs and raid the larder. He didn't care that in the morning everyone else had to go without their breakfast.

At last, in desperation, Dick's mother went to see Saint Ulric.

'What can I do with him?' she asked. 'I love him, he's my son, but I don't like the way he has become greedy and selfish. He doesn't care if the rest of us go hungry, even the little ones, just so long as he can eat what he wants.'

'Bring me some bread tomorrow morning,' said Saint Ulric. 'Then send Dick to see me tomorrow afternoon, but don't tell him about the bread.'

That evening Dick's mother baked some bread, and hid it. The next morning she secretly took some to Saint Ulric. He put it on his table, together with two cottage loaves. Then he whispered something in her ear and she nodded.

Later that afternoon, Dick was sent to see Saint Ulric.

'Come in,' said Ulric. 'I want you to do something for me. I want you to take all the bread on my table to your mother. Now be quick about it. I have things to do!'

Dick stared at the loaves on the table. He recognised the long crusty loaf as one of his mother's. She always baked loaves like that. But why was it here? It must be the one she'd baked last night, the one he'd spent hours searching for. Why was Saint Ulric asking him to take it back to her?

Dick suddenly felt afraid. He grabbed the three loaves off the table and ran outside as fast as he could. But outside again in the sunshine, he wondered why he'd felt so scared. It was only bread. His mother wouldn't know how many loaves he was supposed to take home. Dick ate one of the cottage loaves. Then he ate the other. He nibbled at his mother's loaf, and soon that was eaten too.

By the time Dick arrived home, he was feeling ill because he'd eaten all the bread, and guilty for the same reason. He sat on the step outside the back door and clutched his stomach.

'Oh hello,' said his mother. 'I didn't know you were sitting there. Here, I've got something for you,' and she handed him a big white crust of bread, covered in butter and strawberry jam.

'That's for being a good boy and bringing me the three loaves from Saint Ulric,' she said.

'Three loaves?' said Dick, suddenly feeling afraid again.

'Yes,' said his mother. 'I don't know why you sound so surprised. You put them on the table only a few minutes ago. Look!' and she pointed to a long crusty loaf sitting on the table next to two crisp cottage loaves.

'But... But I ate them,' said Dick. 'No you didn't,' laughed his mother. 'You can't have done, because they're here on the table. Anyway', she added, 'You wouldn't do that, would you. You wouldn't eat the bread that you'd been asked to bring home to me. You're a good boy Dick. You're not greedy are you?'

'No,' said Dick. And the strange thing was, that from that day on, Dick was *not* greedy or selfish again.

How the Manx cat lost her tail   *Odedience*
adapted from Manx mythology

At the beginning of time when the world was new, the Manx cat had a tail. It was a fine tail, a long tail, a tail ringed with stripes like that of a tiger, a tail to be proud of.

The Manx cat was a proud animal. She walked tall with her tail held high; except when she was stalking her prey – then she held it low, level with the ground, so as not to be seen by her victim; or when she was sleeping, when she curled her tail tightly around her body, and buried her head into its soft fur.

The Manx cat was an independent animal. She liked to go her own way, follow her own instinct, make her own decisions without being told what to do by others. But her independence got her into trouble one day.

It was at the time of the great flood. God was displeased with the people on earth. He was unhappy with the way they behaved, with the way they treated each other, with the way they treated the earth itself.

'They must be taught a lesson,' said God.

He spoke to Noah, and told him to build an ark: a boat big enough to hold two of each animal and all Noah's family. The work was almost finished. The ark was almost ready.

God spoke to all the creatures.

'You must go to the ark. Two by two. All of you. Noah will show you the place that is yours. He will care for you until the flood is over. Go now. Steadily. Quietly. Quickly. Before the rain starts.'

The animals set off for the ark. Two of each kind, together, towards the boat that would keep them safe throughout the storm to come. But one animal didn't want to listen.

'I have things to do,' said the Manx cat. 'I have hunting to do, mice to catch, I can't come.' And she carried on stalking mice in the grass.

The other animals went on board the ark. They were shown their places by Noah and his family. The ark filled with the sound and sight and scent of animals. The first few drops of rain fell.

'Come on,' called Noah to the animals still going into the ark. 'No time to lose. The rain is here. Come on.' The animals hurried.

'And you,' called Noah to the Manx cat. 'Don't be late. Don't get left behind. Come now.'

'I'm not ready,' said the Manx cat. 'I'll come when I want, not when *you* want. I have things to do just now,' and she carried on washing her whiskers.

Noah ushered the last of the animals into the ark. The rain fell more heavily.

'Come *along*,' called Noah again to the Manx cat. 'If you don't come now, you'll get left behind,' and Noah turned to go into the ark. He and his sons pulled up the heavy ramp they had used as a footpath for the animals. Noah's wife and his daughters closed all the shutters against the rain. Noah began to close the door.

The Manx cat felt rain on her fur. It was heavy, persistent, cold rain. She felt it soak into her coat, and she felt afraid. She suddenly knew she had been foolish not to obey Noah. She realised that if she didn't go into the ark with the other animals she would drown in the flood.

She sprang towards the ark and leapt on to it. She squeezed into the tiny gap in the closing door. It shut with a snap, and trapped her tail. The Manx cat cried out in pain, and Noah released her, but too late to save her beautiful tail, her fine long tail ringed with stripes like a tiger. The manx cat had lost her tail because she didn't come when she was called.

Jack o'Kent, the Devil and the pigs   *Honesty/consideration for animals*
adapted from Welsh folk-legend

There was once a man called Jack o'Kent, who went to market to buy some pigs. The Devil was also there, also buying pigs.

'Why don't you have these?' said the Devil to Jack, pointing to some ill, thin animals.

'I'm after strong, healthy pigs,' said Jack o'Kent. 'I don't want sickly creatures that are going to die as soon as I get them home.'

'Then what about these?' said the Devil, showing Jack some sorry-looking animals.

'No, I don't want those either,' said Jack o'Kent. 'You leave me alone to choose my pigs myself. You buy yours, and I'll buy mine. Now go away.'

But the Devil wouldn't go away. He pestered and bothered and annoyed and irritated Jack o'Kent, until he was quite angry.

'Go away!' he said. 'Leave me alone!'

'I'll make a bargain with you,' said the Devil. 'You buy your pigs, and I'll buy mine, but whichever of us has pigs with the curliest tails in the morning, can pay for the pigs of the other.'

'I don't know what you mean,' said Jack.

'I mean that if my pigs have curlier tails than yours in the morning, you can pay for my pigs.'

'And if my pigs have the curliest tails, you will pay for mine?' said Jack o'Kent.

'Yes,' said the Devil. 'But you won't win!' and he smiled to himself because he knew he was going to cheat to win.

So Jack o'Kent and the Devil agreed to meet each other in the market square in the morning, and they both went away to choose their pigs.

By now, the pigs for sale in the market place were tired and hungry. They looked dejected and despondent and depressed. Their tails had lost their curl and were drooping and straight. Jack o'Kent knew his pigs were hungry and tired, so he took them to a spare pig-pen and bought fresh clean straw for them to lie on. Then he went and found water for them, and bought food for them to eat. Having done all that, he curled up with them on the straw, to protect them from harm in the night. Then he went to sleep.

The Devil meanwhile, had taken his pigs to an empty pig-pen. But he didn't hurry away to buy straw and food and water, he hurried off to buy a pair of curling tongs. He dragged each pig towards him in turn, and tried to curl its tail with the tongs.

'That Jack o'Kent will never beat me,' he said. 'Whatever he does to his pigs it'll not curl their tails as much as my curling tongs. I'll win, and he'll have to pay me.'

The Devil spent all night trying to curl his pigs' tails with the tongs, but by morning, the tails were still drooping limp and straight, and the pigs were restless and unhappy with lack of food and sleep.

'Well, it's the best I can do,' said the Devil, as he drove his pigs out of the pen and back towards the market place to meet Jack o'Kent.

When he got there, the Devil could hardly believe his eyes. There was Jack, surrounded by lively, frisky, playful pigs, looking fresh and healthy, and every one with the curliest tail the Devil had ever seen.

'How did you do that?' demanded the Devil. 'You must have cheated. Pigs never have tails as curly as that!'

'Oh yes they do,' said Jack o'Kent. 'At least they do when they're well cared for. You were so busy trying to cheat me, and win the money, that you forgot about looking after the pigs. You deserve to lose if you try to cheat, and you deserve to lose if you don't look after your animals properly.'

The Devil knew he was beaten and he offered Jack o'Kent the money he owed him.

'No,' said Jack. 'I don't want your money. But I'll take your pigs, and I'll look after them as they should be looked after.' So Jack o'Kent took his own pigs and those of the Devil, and looked after them all and cared for them well.

The students who boasted   *Conceit/think before you speak/tolerance*
adapted from British folk-lore

A famous professor once went to visit the students of a certain town. The professor was known to be very wise, very clever, very well-read and very knowledgeable, and the students of the town were anxious to show him that they too were intelligent and well-educated.

'We are the cleverest people in Britain,' they boasted. 'We want him to know that. And we want him to think that everyone in our town is brilliant.' So some of the students dressed up as farm workers and road menders, hay makers and tree cutters, and pretended to be doing those jobs on the roads that led to the town centre.

Soon the professor came by in his carriage and met a group of people mending the road.

'Hello!' he called. 'Can you tell me if this is the way to the town centre?' The road menders answered him very politely in Latin.

'Goodness me!' thought the professor. 'The people around here are very clever.' He drove a little further and saw a group of workers digging a ditch at the side of a field.

'Is this the way to the university?' he asked. The workers answered him very politely in Greek.

'Well! I didn't realise that the people here are so well-educated,' said the professor to himself. 'If the workers are as clever as this, the students must be brilliant! I shall have to rethink the examination I was going to give them.'

When he arrived at the university, the professor announced to the students that he had changed his mind.

'I was going to examine you in Latin and Greek and French and German,' he said. 'But I think that will be too easy for you. So I have decided to examine you in the language of signs – in a language using no words. That will show me how clever you *really* are.'

The students looked worried. 'But we don't know how to communicate using signs,' they whispered to each other. 'What are we going to do?'

Just then, the town miller came walking past and the students said, 'We'll send him instead of us. When he gets the exam all wrong, we can truthfully say it's not our fault.' And before the poor miller had time to find out what was going on, he was bundled into the examination room, and found himself standing in front of the very important professor.

The students waited anxiously outside. What was going to happen? What would the professor say when he found out he was examining an ordinary miller, and not a clever student?

Minutes went by. Suddenly the door of the room burst open.

'What a clever chap,' said the professor, clapping the miller on the back. 'He is without a doubt the cleverest man I have ever met. He understood what all my signs were.'

'I showed him an apple, which represented the fall of mankind. He showed me a piece of bread, to represent the Bread of Life.

'I held up one finger to show the power of God. He held up another to show that God is also Christ.

'I held up three fingers to represent the Holy Trinity. He held up his clenched fist to show that The Trinity is but One God.

'He is indeed the cleverest man!'

The students stared at the miller in disbelief. 'How did you do it?' they whispered. 'How did you know what all the signs meant?'

'I knew what the signs meant, all right,' said the miller in an angry voice. 'He pushed an apple under my nose, so I shoved a crust of bread under his. Then he poked a finger at me, so I poked a finger at him. Then, he poked three fingers in my face. I'm not standing for that, so I shook my fist at him. He's the rudest man I ever met,' and the miller walked out of the room.

'I think they've misunderstood each other,' said one of the students. 'I think it was our fault. We shouldn't have boasted in the first place, and we shouldn't have pushed the miller into the exam with the professor.'

And the students agreed never to do anything like it again.

The section of this story dealing with the conversation in sign language can be traced as far back as the 13th century. The theme has been used by various writers including Rabelais, and a version is also found in the Islamic Nasrudin stories.

The greedy landlord　　　　*Greed/dishonesty/doing your best/selfishness*
adapted from Irish folk-lore

There was once a man who owned an inn. He was a greedy, selfish, dishonest man, who was only interested in making a profit and getting rich. But despite everything he did, the inn became more and more run down, and the man became poorer and poorer.

One day, the man's uncle came to visit him. The two of them hadn't met for quite some time.

'Well, how are you Tom, and how's business?' asked the uncle.

'Oh, things are bad,' said Tom. 'In fact, they couldn't be worse. I'm getting poorer every day even thought I'm doing everything I can to make money. I've put water in all the barrels of beer, to make it go further. I've watered down all the wine as well. I buy the cheapest meat and vegetables for the customers' meals (but I still charge them the highest prices). I give them the wrong change whenever I can, so that I make more money. But still I'm poor. I don't know what's wrong.'

'I think I do,' said his uncle. 'Come with me.'

Tom's uncle took him to the store room where all the beer, wine, and food was kept. He opened the door a little, and said 'Now, look in there. What do you see.'

Tom looked, but could see nothing out of the ordinary, nothing different from what he saw every day when he looked into the store room.

'I don't see anything,' said Tom.

'No, I don't suppose you do,' said his uncle. 'But if you put your foot on my foot, and your hand on my head, you'll be able to see what I can see.'

Tom did what his uncle said, then looked again into the store room. This time he could hardly believe his eyes. There in the middle of the store room floor sat a small fat man. He was stuffing himself with food. He gorged on cakes and butter, salt and flour, ham and wine, eggs and beer, all at the same time.

'What is it?' said Tom.

'It's a buttery spirit,' said his uncle. 'They live in inns where there's greed and dishonesty. They thrive where there's cheating and laziness.'

'But what can I do about it?' said Tom. 'How can I get rid of it?'

'You can't,' said his uncle. 'As long as you are cheating your customers, the buttery spirit will cheat you. Of course, if you change your ways and start giving your customers value for money, then the buttery spirit may well go away. But you'll need to give the best food and drink for your prices, not the cheap food and watered down drink that you're giving now.'

And with that, Tom's uncle said he was leaving, but that he would visit again soon.

Several weeks went by, and the weeks turned into months. Tom's uncle didn't return. But Tom was making changes to his inn. And as the changes were made, Tom's profits grew. He was becoming a rich man. His inn was always full of customers. People came from far and near to taste Tom's delicious meals, to have a jar of his famous beer, or a glass of his tasty wine, or to have a room for the night – a good night's sleep in a clean and comfortable bed.

A year went by. Tom's uncle came back.

'Well, how are you Tom, and how's business?' asked the uncle.

'Couldn't be better,' smiled Tom. 'Things are wonderful. The inn is always full of customers, and my purse is full of money!'

'And what about the buttery spirit?' asked his uncle.

'I don't know,' said Tom. 'Shall we go and see?'

They went to the store room and opened the door a crack. Tom put a foot on his uncle's foot, and a hand on his head. They peeped together into the room. There in the middle of the floor sat a tiny, thin, weak, wizened, ill-looking buttery spirit. He was trying to eat a currant bun, but hadn't the strength to lift it to his mouth.

'There you are, you see,' said Tom's uncle. 'They don't thrive in a place where there's honesty and hard work. It won't last much longer now, unless of course you go back to your old ways.'

'Oh no,' said Tom. 'I've learned that hard work and honest ways get the best profits in the end.'

The Hedley Kow   *Cheerfulness in adversity*
adapted from Yorkshire folk-lore

There was once an old woman who lived in the village of Hedley in Yorkshire. She was a widow. She lived all alone, had little money, few possessions, no family, was often hungry or cold or both; yet in spite of all this she was always cheerful and optimistic. She always had time for a smile and a friendly word.

One day the old woman was walking home from visiting a friend, when she spotted an old iron pot in the hedge-bottom.

'That's a lucky find,' she said to herself. 'Even if it has a hole in it, it'll do as a flower pot. I'll take it home.'

The pot didn't seem to belong to anyone. It wasn't near anyone's house or garden, so the old woman picked it up and set of home again. But with every step she took, the pot seemed to get heavier and heavier. At last the old woman could carry it no longer and she dropped it on the ground.

To her astonishment, gold pieces spilled out of it.

'Well I never!' she said. 'It certainly is my lucky day today. I'll be as rich as a queen with all that lot.'

The woman pondered how she was going to carry the pot home, now that it was so heavy.

'I'll drag it along behind me,' she thought. So she took off her shawl, tied it round the handle of the pot, and pulled it along behind her. Soon she was out of breath. She stopped for a rest and the pot stopped too, falling over and spilling out silver coins on to the ground.

'That's funny,' she said. 'I was sure they were golden pieces. Never mind. Silver's probably better. Anyway, it's prettier.'

She tied the shawl a little more tightly round the handle of the pot, and set off again. But soon the pot began bumping along the ground much more roughly than before. The old woman turned round to see why, and could hardly believe her eyes. The pot of bright shining silver coins had turned into a bar of rusty old iron.

'Well! Lawks a mercy me!' she said. 'And I was sure it was a pot of silver. Still, an iron bar's better. The silver might have got stolen. No-one's going to steal an iron bar, but I can sell it to the scrapman and be a few pence better off than I was this morning before I found it.'

The old woman tied her shawl tightly round the iron bar, and trudged on homewards. Soon she came to her door, and turned round to hoist the iron bar up the step and over the threshold. But, lo and behold, it had gone and in its place was a large round stone.

'Well! Fancy that!' said the woman. 'And I was sure it was an iron bar. Still, a stone's better. It's exactly the right shape and size for me to use to hold my door open in the summer, to stop it banging shut. It certainly is my lucky day today.'

The old woman bent down to untie her shawl from the stone, when suddenly it moved. It wriggled and jiggled and shuddered and juddered. Then out of it shot four long lanky legs, a head with two ears and two horns, a topknot of curly hair, and a tail with a silky tassel on the end.

'Well, my goodness me!' said the woman, as she burst out laughing. 'The Hedley Kow. To think that I've lived in these parts all my life and I've never seen it before.'

The Hedley Kow, for that's what the creature was – a mischievous fun-loving practical joker – kicked its legs out, swished its tail, tossed its head, and leapt in the air, before galloping off down the lane, mooing as it went. 'It's surely been my lucky day today,' said the old woman. 'I've not laughed so much for ages. Just think! The Hedley Kow. Fancy that!' And she went into her cottage feeling grand.

The twelve men of Gotham   *What you look for may be under your nose*
adapted from British folk-lore

The men of Gotham thought themselves to be clever and wise. They thought they understood the world and everything in it. They believed that they were special people, and probably they were.

One day, twelve men of Gotham went fishing. The day was bright and sunny, and the fishing was good. They'd had an early start in the morning, and now it was almost evening. Almost time to go home.

'We ought to check that we are all safe and sound,' said one man of Gotham. 'After all, we have been on and near and by and in the river all day. One of us might have slipped and fallen in.'

'That could have happened,' said the other men of Gotham. 'One of us could have drowned without the others knowing. We must check to see that we are all here.'

The twelve men of Gotham lined up at the river's edge. They had their fishing rods, lines, nets and baskets with them. They also had the day's catch; and a very good catch it was. Over a hundred fish to take back home. A hundred fish to share between the families.

The first man of Gotham acted as spokesperson and counter. He started counting the men at the first one in the line.

'One, two, three, four, five, six, seven, eight, nine, ten, eleven,' he counted. There was panic.

'Where is the twelfth one of us,' cried the men. 'One of us is missing. One of us is drowned. Oh what an unhappy day this is.'

'No, that can't be so,' said the second man of Gotham. 'I'm sure we are all here. I'll count.'

The second man of Gotham made all the others line up straight and still, at the water's edge. He too, began to count.

'One, two, three, four, five, six, seven, eight, nine, ten, eleven,' he said. There was panic.

'It's true,' the men shouted. 'One of us is lost. This is the saddest day.'

'No, no,' said the third man of Gotham. 'We are all here, I am sure. Let me count.' So the third man of Gotham counted the fishermen.

'One, two, three, four, five, six, seven, eight, nine, ten, eleven. It's true,' he said quietly. 'One of us is indeed missing.'

The fourth man of Gotham tried to count the men. Then the fifth had a turn, the sixth counted, the seventh tried, and so on, until all twelve men had counted his comrades. All twelve men came to the same conclusion. One of their friends had drowned.

The men of Gotham were inconsolable. They cried and shouted, wept and howled. They searched for the missing man, they waded into the river to try and find his body. But it was nowhere to be seen.

In the middle of all the commotion, a small boy came by.

'What's the matter?' he asked.

The first man of Gotham explained the situation.

'But you're all here!' said the boy.

'No. We thought we were, but we're not,' said the men.

'What if I find your missing friend?' asked the boy.

'Would you? Could you?' said the men. 'We'll give you all our fish if only you can find the missing man.'

The boy asked them all to line up again. He asked them to count every time they felt a blow. The men agreed to do that. The boy went up to the first man and struck him hard on the chest. The man shouted 'one'. The boy went to the second man and trod on his toe. The man called 'two'. The boy went to the third man, and the fourth and so on, each one counting, each one feeling the boy's hand or foot, until the twelfth man shouted 'twelve'.

'He's found the man who was missing!' said the twelve men of Gotham. 'Thank you. Oh thank you. Here, take our fish,' and the grateful men gave the small boy their entire day's catch of a hundred fish.

'Thank you,' said the boy. 'They're the easiest fish I've ever caught. You could have saved yourselves your supper if you'd looked a little more closely.'

But the clever men of Gotham didn't understand what the boy meant.

cf. 'The man who lost himself' page 100, in which a man fails to find himself when he looks in his bed.

The Seagull   *Doing your best*
adapted from a Manx fable

There was once a young seagull, who found himself clinging to the side of a cliff, all alone. His mother and father had not returned from a hunting expedition. He didn't know what to do. He looked down at the heaving sea below him and wondered if there was food to eat down there. But it was a long drop. The sea looked angry. He was sure he would be killed.

'Better to stay where I am,' thought the seagull.

But as soon as he had decided to stay put, the jutting piece of rock on which he was sitting, gave way and plunged down to the water, taking the young seagull with it. The rock splashed into the sea, and the seagull found himself bobbing about on the waves. He looked around for something to eat, but could see nothing.

'I'm going to starve as well as drown,' he thought gloomily.

Just then, a mackerel popped up out of the waves.

'Are you all alone?' it asked.

'Yes,' the seagull said. 'I've lost my mother and father and I don't know what to do.'

'Just do your best and try your hardest,' said the mackerel, and with a flash of blue and silver scales, it was gone beneath the waves again.

The seagull was not sure what the mackerel meant, so he went on looking for something to eat. Suddenly he saw a tiny insect darting across the water.

'Do your best,' said the seagull to himself, as he dived after the insect. It tasted good. There were more, and soon the seagull was full and satisfied.

While he had been feeding on the insects, the waves and tide had been carrying the young gull further and further out to sea. He noticed how far he was from the shoreline and the cliffs, and he panicked.

'I will surely drown,' he called, and he swam and swam with all his strength, as he tried to regain the land. It was no use. His strength was nothing compared to the sea's.

'What's the matter baby gull?' asked a herring swimming by. 'You look all in a panic.'

'I'm being swept away,' cried the seagull, 'and I don't know what to do.'

'Fishes swim and gulls fly,' said the herring wisely. 'Just do your best and try your hardest,' and he disappeared under the swell of the sea.

'Fishes swim and gulls fly!' murmured the gull, and he stretched out his wings, flapped them a few times, and found himself soaring over the waves towards the land. It wasn't a perfect flight, being only his first, but it delivered him safely to the rocks again. He landed, somewhat abruptly, at the feet of a great black shag, who was hanging his wings out to dry in the sun.

'What's the matter little gull?' asked the black shag. 'Can't you find enough fish to eat.'

'Fish?' said the seagull. 'I don't know how to fish.'

'Just do your best and try your hardest,' said the shag, and with a flap and flurry of black feathers, he dived into the sea, emerging with a silver fish speared on his long beak.

The seagull peered into the waves and saw a tiny flash of silver. He dived with hardly a splash and came up with a small fish in his beak. In a quick swallow it was gone. He soared into the air again and shouted thanks to the great shag. The wind picked up his cry and carried it over the rocks and sea.

'The young gull has found his voice,' said the swans who were swimming down river. 'But he'll lose it soon, for there's a storm coming. It'll be too fierce for the likes of him.'

The young seagull had not noticed the gathering storm clouds, the whining wind, or the white caps on the waves. He had not met a storm before, but soon he was blown back to the water, buffeted by the waves, stung with sea spray. He was half drowned when he heard the chug of an engine and saw a flock of gulls following a fishing boat back to harbour.

'Just do your best and try your hardest,' cried the gulls. 'Follow us.'

The young gull fought to escape from the heavy wet hold of the sea. He dragged his waterlogged wings from the waves, and half swimming, half flying, followed the boat. Then, with a final burst of energy, he flew up to the rigging of the boat and clung on until it reached harbour.

When the boat was safely moored, the seagulls flocked round, screeching and squabbling, to steal the fish as it was unloaded and packed in ice. The little seagull realised that here was a good place to live. Here was food in plenty, and friends as well.

He made his home in the harbour. Sometimes he met the fishing boats as they returned from sea, sometimes he fished for himself. Sometimes he took the food that the men and women threw to the gulls. He became strong and bold, fearless and brave, and life was good.

One day a baby gull looked up to him and said, 'How do I grow to be brave and bold like you?'

'Just do your best and try your hardest,' said the seagull, but he didn't tell the little one that it was a broken rock that had launched him on his first flight into the world.

The man from Ballasalla
adapted from Manx folk-lore

What you look for may be under your nose

There was once a man from Ballasalla who wanted to see the world.

'I need to see what there is to see, ' he said to his wife. 'I'll not be able to see what I can see, sitting here at my own fire-side.' So he packed a few things into a knapsack and set off to see the world.

He hadn't gone far when he met a local farmer.

'Hello John,' called the farmer. 'And where are you off to with your knapsack on your back?'

'I'm going to see the world,' said John.

'There are beautiful things to see in the world, or so I'm told,' said the farmer.

'Yes, but if it's beauty you're after, you'll find plenty in Ballasalla,' said John.

'Well, it's you who's off to see the world,' laughed the farmer, and he went on his way.

A few minutes later the man from Ballasalla met a neighbour coming home from market.

'Morning John' she said. 'And where'll you be going this fine day?'

'I'm off to see the world,' said John. 'To see what I can see.'

'I had a brother once went travelling,' said the woman. 'He came back and told us tales of the most wonderful foreign food he'd eaten. Delicious he said it was.'

'If it's delicious food you're after,' said John, 'You don't have to go far away from Ballasalla.'

'Well, it's you who's off to see the world,' said the neighbour, and she walked on, smiling to herself.

Towards evening, the man from Ballasalla arrived at Doolish, and what a fine place it was. The town buzzed with people and carriages, the sea sparkled, the harbour was alive with boats and ships and comings and goings and landings and loadings.

A sailor, who'd been born in Ballasalla, suddenly saw John.

'Hey,' he shouted. 'How are things back home? How are you? What are you doing?'

'I'm off to see the world,' answered John.

'And a wonderful time you'll have,' said the sailor. 'The world is a remarkable place. You'll love it. Which ship are you travelling on? Where are you bound?'

'I'm not going on a ship,' said John. 'No. Why do I need to set foot on foreign soil, when there's lots of soil round Ballasalla I've not yet trodden on?'

'Please yourself,' laughed the sailor. 'But it's you who said you were going to see the world.'

John walked on. It was getting dark now, and the road was lonely and hard. He began to wish he was back at home in his own kitchen, sitting down to a dinner cooked by his wife. He realised it was some time since he'd eaten anything.

Suddenly, rising out of the gloom in front of him, John saw a glittering silvery palace. He could smell food and he could hear people talking. A woman appeared in front of him.

'Come in John,' she said. 'Come and eat and drink with us. Come and rest your weary bones.' She held out her skinny fingers towards him, but John felt afraid. He knew better than to go to a stranger's place.

'No thanks,' said John. 'I don't hear the people in there saying grace. We don't sit down to dinner in Ballasalla without saying grace first, so I'll not join you. Thank you all the same.'

The strange silver palace dissolved in the mist, and John was left alone on the road. By now the dark had closed in around him, and the mist swirled more thickly.

John walked steadily on.

A noise to his left, made John turn and stumble. There stood the Buggane, a wicked shape-shifting bogey-beast, up to no good. It held up its enormous arms to signal John to stop.

'No,' said John. 'A man from Ballasalla won't give way to you. A Ballasalla man is not to be stopped by evil and wickedness,' and he kept on walking. The Buggane, angered by John's lack of fear, took off its head and threw it on the ground in front of John, in a shower of coloured sparks. Then, with a flash, it was back on its shoulders.

'If you want to see fireworks,' said John calmly, 'You should come to Ballasalla in November.' The Buggane was so annoyed that he had been unable to scare this man, that he disappeared in a puff of smoke.

John kept on walking. In the dark mist he had little idea where he was, but he suddenly spotted a house he recognised. Its lighted windows looked familiar and he walked towards it. His wife came to the door.

'I've seen the world,' said John, 'And some fine strange things there are in it. But,' he added, 'The world is pretty much like Ballasalla in many ways, though Ballasalla's better!'

Further reading

For teachers
Christianity P. Moore (Lutterworth Educational 1982)
Comparative Religions ed. W. Owen Cole (Blandford Press 1982)
Jesus A.N. Wilson (Sinclair-Stevenson 1992)
Jesus and the Four Gospels John Drane (Lion 1979)
Six Religions in the Twentieth Century W. Owen Cole with Peggy Morgan
   (Hulton Educational 1984)

The Christians Bamber Gascoigne (BBC)

The Orthodox Way Kallistos Ware (Mowbray 1979)

A Sampler of British Folk-Tales Katharine M. Briggs (Routledge & Kegan Paul 1977)

English Fables and Fairy Stories James Reeves (Oxford University Press, first printed 1954, reprinted 1972)

Fairy Tales from the Isle of Man Dora Broome (Penguin Books 1953, reprinted Norris Modern Press Ltd 1980)

Folk-Lore and Legends of England (first published 1890 reprinted by EP Publishing Ltd 1972)

In Search of Lost Gods – A Guide to British Folklore Ralph Whitlock (Phaidon Press 1979)

Manx Fairy Tales Sophia Morrison (first published 1929, reprinted by The Manx Experience 1991)

For children

I am a Greek Orthodox/Roman Catholic/Anglican/Pentecostal 'My Belief' Series (Franklin Watts)

Learning About the Church Felicity Henderson (Lion Books 1984)

Stories from the Christian World (Macdonald 1987)

The Christian World Alan Brown (Macdonald 1984)

The Living Festivals Series – Christmas, Shrove Tuesday and Ash Wednesday, Holy Week, Easter, Hallowe'en, All Souls & All Saints (RMEP 1982).

Useful addresses

British & Foreign Bible Society, Stonehill Green, Westlea, Swindon SN5 7DG

British Council of Churches, 1 Eaton Gate, London SW1W 9BT

Christian Aid, PO Box 1, London SW1.

Christian Education Movement, Royal Buildings Victoria Street, Derby DE1 1GW

National Christian Education Council, Robert Denholm House, Nutfield, Redhill, Surrey RH1 4HW

Scripture Union, 130 City Road, London EC1V 2NJ

Hinduism

Hinduism is the world's oldest major religion and is the name given to the religion and way of life of a group of people who settled in the Indus Valley in India around 2500 BCE. It is one of only two religions (the other is Judaism) which pre-dates human beings' ability to write. The world's oldest Holy Book – the Rig Veda – was in existence by about 1000 BCE.

Hinduism is the third largest religion in the world, and has about 550 million followers. An estimated 300,000 Hindus live in Britain, many of whom have emigrated here during this century.

Hinduism is believed to have come to the west via the teaching of Vivekananda (1863-1902) a disciple of Ramakrishna who was a popular religious leader of the 19th century. Ramakrishna taught by way of simple stories, and accepted the truths of other religions. Ramakrishna died before becoming well known, but Vivekananda resolved to continue his work and to extend it by encouraging Hindus to rid themselves of social injustices and aim towards a more egalitarian society.

After the First World War Asians, Sikhs, Muslims, and Hindus came to Britain as traders. In the industrial boom of the 1950s, British employers recruited in India, Pakistan, East Africa and the Caribbean when they could not attract native Britons to jobs in textiles, engineering, hospitals and public transport.

Hinduism is said to be more a culture than a creed. It has no founder and no prophet. It emphasises experiences rather than history; a way of living rather than a way of thought. What counts is conduct rather than belief. The moral laws teach modesty, kindness, honesty, truthfulness and hospitality. The caste system determined which groups of the community should do which duties, but the system was made illegal in 1947.

Hindus believe in one supreme God – Brahman, the essence of the universe. God has no beginning and no end, is neither man nor woman, encompasses the entire universe, yet is also so small as to be incomprehensible to man. God is infinite, omnipresent and omnipotent, but because of the complexity of the breadth of God, Hindus believe that he may appear to different people in different forms, and that there are many different ways of reaching him. Hindus therefore pay respect to many different Gods, whom they believe are all aspects of the one supreme being. Hinduism is thus extraordinarily diverse, and the attitude of tolerance towards each Hindu's personal or chosen God extends to tolerance of other religions. Historically, Hindus have rarely been at war because of religious differences.

Hinduism has been described as a deep flowing river, into which, over a period of more than three thousand years, many streams have flowed. However, Hinduism has certain discernible features:

- the belief that the spirit of God – Brahman – is present in all living things
- the belief that it is wrong to harm any living thing,
- the belief in reincarnation – that the soul is reborn in another body until it is released from the cycle of birth, death and rebirth by achieving the highest state – Moshka – through a perfect life
- the belief in Karma – that a person's actions and conduct in one life will determine their next; that poor conduct leads to a rebirth in the lower orders, and that good actions lead to rebirth in the higher orders

The fables in this section of *Share our World* are adapted from the *Panchatantra* – a collection of Hindu stories written originally in Sanskrit, and dating from somewhere between 100 BCE and 500 CE.

Panchatantra means five books, and the collection comprises stories within a story. In the book as a whole, a wise priest attempts to instruct three rather dull and foolish princes in the art of worldly wisdom. But beware! The 'morals' of the stories are sometimes immoral in our eyes; they have no bearing on morality as such. They praise shrewdness and worldly wisdom in life and in politics.

The original *Panchatantra* is no longer in existence, neither is its first translation into Pahlavi, believed to have been made in the sixth century. However, in about 750 CE the Pahlavi version was translated into Arabic and entitled 'Kalilah and Dimnah'. Further translations were made into Greek, Hebrew, Latin and Spanish. From these five translations, versions were later written in Italian, French, German and English. The first English version was published in London in 1570, and later known as 'The Fables of Bidpai'.

There are now more than 200 different versions of the *Panchatantra* in more than 50 languages. The stories remain very popular in India, and are retold again and again in verse, and prose, and translated into old language and modern idiom. Many of the stories have entered into the folk-lore of the story-loving Hindus and have reappeared in modern collections of traditional oral tales. It is argued that no other work of Hindu literature has played such an important part in world literature as the *Panchatantra*.

The birds choose a king
adapted from the Panchatantra Book Three

Think before you speak

Once, almost at the very beginning of time, the birds had no king. They decided they ought to have a leader, a ruler, a protector, a chief, a boss; in short... a king. They called a meeting of every bird they could find, and, after a great deal of discussion, they chose the owl as their king.

'We think you should be our leader because you are wise, you can think. We want you to be king. Will you do it?'

'Yes,' said the owl. 'I will be pleased to be king.'

So the birds collected together all the things they needed for the coronation, and prepared to crown the owl as their king and leader.

They seated him on a royal throne covered in velvet cushions and they brought a beautiful golden crown to put on his head.

One bird was chosen to place the crown on the owl's head, and he was just about to do so and to declare the owl king, when a crow flew past.

The birds stopped the coronation ceremony and whispered between themselves, 'We must have forgotten to ask the crow to the meeting to choose the king. But it's not right that he hasn't had chance to say what he thinks. Let's ask him now.'

The birds turned to the crow and one of them said 'Do you agree with us that the owl should be crowned king of all the birds?' But much to their surprise, the crow said 'No! I don't!'

'Oh!' said the birds. 'Why not?'

'Well,' said the crow, 'Why haven't you chosen the swan, or the duck, or the peacock, or the cuckoo, or the pigeon, or the parrot, or indeed anyone else? Why have you chosen the owl?'

'Well,' began the birds, 'You see...' But they didn't have chance to say anything else because the crow interrupted them.

'I mean, just look at him,' said the crow. 'He's so ugly. He's squint-eyed, and crooked-nosed. He looks fierce and unfriendly. And if he looks like that now, on his coronation day, when he's supposed to be happy, what on earth is he going to look like when he's angry? How can you have someone who looks like him as king? His face is enough to put anyone off! Oh no! You can't possibly have anyone who looks as ugly as him to be the king of the birds.'

The birds listened to the words of the crow, and decided that perhaps they had been wrong to choose the owl. 'We'll put off the coronation,' they said. 'We'll have another meeting another day, and we'll think again about this important matter of who should be king.' And with that, they all went away to their own homes, and the owl was left sitting by himself on the throne with the velvet cushions, with only the crow for company.

'Why did you do that?' he asked the crow. 'Why did you say all those nasty things about me and interfere with my coronation? What have I ever done to you that makes you want to say such hurtful things to me? I shall never be able to forget your cruel words. In fact I never want to speak to you again, and you and I will always be enemies!' And the owl flew away feeling very angry and hurt.

The crow stared after the owl. 'Oh dear!' he said. 'I didn't mean to do that. I didn't mean to upset you. I didn't want us to fall out,' but the owl was by now far away, and couldn't hear the crow's words.

'Oh dear!' said the crow again. 'I think I've been very stupid. I shouldn't have been rude to him. I shouldn't have said all those nasty things about him. It's silly to fall out with people on purpose. It's unkind to say nasty things about people to hurt them. It's silly to speak without thinking first. And now I don't know what to do to put it right.'

And the crow flew away still wondering what to do about the hurt he had caused.

cf. 'The owl as king' in the Jataka Tales *(the Uluka-Jataka). In this version, the owl and the crow fought, and the birds chose a golden mallard as their king. In Aesop's version of the story 'The peacock and the jackdaw', the peacock is chosen to be king, but the jackdaw objects on the grounds that he will be unable to defend the birds if the eagle attacks.*

The partridge, the hare, and the cat

Settle differences/ choose advisers wisely

adapted from the Panchatantra Book Three

Once upon a time there was a tree that was home to a large number of creatures. Birds lived in its branches, insects lived in the cracks of the trunk, and small mammals lived in the ground under the tree.

Hidden in the grass by the base of the tree trunk was a hole that had once been made by a family of rabbits, but they had moved on and the hole was now empty. Empty, that is, until a partridge moved in.

'This looks like a good home for me,' said the partridge. 'Does anyone mind if I move in here?' No-one seemed to mind, so the partridge moved in.

He was a good neighbour to the other animals. He was there if anyone needed help, he was friendly and kind, he talked when they wanted to chat, but he didn't take his new friends for granted, and he was never a nuisance to anyone.

'He's nice,' the other animals said. 'We're glad he moved in to our tree.'

All went well, until one day, the partridge went out, and simply didn't come back.

'Where is he?' asked the others.

'Is he all right?'

'I wonder if something's happened to him?'

'I wonder if he's been hurt, or got lost?'

'Perhaps he's been in a fight.'

'Perhaps he's been caught by a hunter in a trap.'

'I wonder if he's just decided to go and live somewhere else. After all, he just turned up here one day, out of the blue, he must have lived somewhere else before he came here.'

'Perhaps he's gone back to where he used to live before.'

'It's funny that he never said he was going.'

But no amount of talking, or wondering, or speculating, or questioning, helped the animals to know what had happened to the partridge.

A few days after the partridge had disappeared, a hare moved in to the hole by the tree trunk where the partridge used to live. The animals were not sure what to do about this.

'What if the partridge comes back, and wants to live in that hole again?' some of them said.

'But it's nothing to do with us,' said others. 'It's not our hole. The partridge isn't living in it any more, so if another animal wants to move in, there's nothing really that we can do about it.' So the animals did nothing, and the hare moved in.

Several days later, the partridge came back.

'What are you doing in my home?' he said to the hare. 'This hole is my house, so please leave now.'

'No,' said the hare. 'It's my home now. You left it, and no-one knew where you'd gone, or if you'd be coming back, so I've moved in. It's mine now.'

'No it's not. It's mine!' said the partridge.

'Not any more. It's mine now!' said the hare.

'It's mine!'

'No! It's mine!'

And so the argument went on, with neither giving way to the other. But at last the partridge had an idea. 'Let's ask the other animals what they think. They know I used to live here, and they know that you're living here now. They can decide what we should do.' But when the partridge and the hare looked round for someone to make a decision, everyone had vanished. No-one, it seemed, wanted to have to decide.

Then the hare saw an old cat sitting a little way away from the tree. 'He looks wise,' said the hare. 'Let's ask the cat to be the judge and decide which one of us should have the hole by the tree trunk as our home.'

So they went, side by side, to see the cat. They stood in front of him and told him the story. They asked him to adjudicate, to choose which one of them should have the hole as his home.

The cat listened in silence. Then he stretched, and yawned, and washed his whiskers, and said 'I'm a little deaf. I couldn't quite catch everything you said. Come a little closer and tell me it again.'

The partridge and the hare did as he asked and moved closer to the cat.

They explained the situation again.

'I'm sorry,' said the cat. 'It's a dreadful nuisance being old, and a bit deaf. I still haven't quite understood everything you said. Come a little closer and tell me it again.'

The partridge and the hare, quite unsuspecting, went a little nearer and told the whole tale again.

'Mmm' said the cat, in a voice as quiet as a purr so that they had to move even closer still to hear him. 'Mmm.' Then quick as a flash, straight as a dart, he pounced. And killed both the partridge and the hare in one swoop.

'Serves them right!' he said. 'They should have chosen their judge more carefully if they wanted to save their skins.'

This story is found in collections by La Fontaine, but describes a weasel and a rabbit who turn to a cat to settle their differences over rights to a home.

cf. 'The otters and the jackal' in the Jataka Tales *(the Dabbhapuppha-Jataka). Two otters caught a fish but couldn't decide which should have it. They appealed to a jackal to help, and he gave the head to one, the tail to the other, and kept the middle for himself! The theme is echoed in 'The two goblins' by La Fontaine, in which the two goblins dispute possession of a magic box, shoes and stick. A man is chosen as arbiter, and promises to distribute the items fairly, but puts on the magic shoes and flies away with the box and stick.*

The elephants, the hares and the moon

The strongest may not be the most clever

adapted from the Panchatantra Book Three

Once upon a time, in the land where the elephants lived, there was a terrible drought. It had not rained for twelve years, and the rivers and streams, ponds and pools, wells and water-holes had all dried up.

'We shall have to find water or we shall all die,' said the elephant king. 'Perhaps there is water further away. Perhaps there are rivers still running in the lands adjoining ours. Perhaps there are lakes and lagoons, swamps and reservoirs in the kingdoms beyond ours. Send out messengers to search for water.'

So the elephant messengers set out north, south, east and west, to search for fresh water.

In several days one of them came back.

'We've found some. Clear, clean, cool, fresh water. A whole deep lakeful. It's nearly as big as the sky. Come and see it. It's not too far from here.'

The elephant king and all his followers set off at great speed to see the wonderful lake of water. The messenger was right – it wasn't too far away.

As soon as the herd of elephants saw the water, they all stampeded down to it.

But, they didn't notice the families of hares who lived in the burrows at the edge of the lake. They didn't see the young hares who were playing outside the burrows. They took no notice of the older hares who were sitting, or sunbathing, or drinking at the water's edge. No. They were interested only in reaching the water. They didn't care how they got there, or who they trod on, or trampled on, in their hurry; and many of the hares were killed, or injured in the stampede.

When the elephants had finished drinking, they climbed from the lake, and set off home again, pleased with themselves for finding water, but oblivious to the fact that they had caused such destruction to the families of hares.

The hares who were still alive and unhurt met together.

'What are we going to do?' they asked. 'The elephants will come again now they know where the lake is. The same thing will happen again. And in no time at all we'll be wiped out. They'll kill us all. They just don't care about anyone but themselves.'

'I will go and see their king,' said the leader of the hares.

'But that's no good,' said one of the others. 'You are so much smaller than them. They'll kill you.'

'No,' said the leader. 'I have an idea. We may be smaller than elephants, but we can think just as well as them, if not better! I have a plan. Leave it to me.'

When it began to get dark, the chief hare set off to see the elephant king. He climbed to the top of a hill near the elephant's home, and called out to him. 'Hello, king of the elephants.'

The elephant king looked round to see who was calling him, and saw the hare on top of the hill.

'What do you want?' he said.

'I am here as a messenger,' said the hare. 'The moon has sent me with a message.'

'The moon?' said the king of the elephants. 'What message?'

'The moon says you have upset him,' said the hare. 'The moon cares for those hares who live near the lake, but he says you have hurt them in your search for water. He says you were wrong to do this. He says that big strong animals should protect smaller animals – not kill and injure them. The moon says you should not go to his lake again to drink, but that you should stay away from it and find another lake to drink from.'

'I'm sorry,' said the elephant king. 'I didn't mean to upset the moon. I didn't hurt the hares on purpose. What can I do to say how sorry I am?'

'Come with me,' said the hare. 'Come with me and you can speak to the moon yourself. You can tell him you're sorry, and you can promise him that you and the other elephants will never come to the lake again.' The hare came down from the hill top and led the elephant king to the lake again.

'There!' said the hare. 'Look into the lake and you will see the moon for yourself.'

The elephant king looked into the lake, and there, sure enough, he could see the pale silver face of the moon, deep in the water.

'But if I tell him we're sorry, surely he'll let us come and drink here again?' said the elephant, and he dipped his trunk into the depths of the lake to take a drink.

As he did so, the face of the moon quivered and trembled. It split into a thousand fragmented pieces and each broken piece of silver shivered and shook in the dark waters.

The elephant stood back, surprised.

'You see what you have done now!' said the hare. 'You've made him even more angry than before. See how he shakes with the anger he feels. If I were you I'd leave now, before he becomes angrier still. Who knows what he might do then?'

'You're right,' said the elephant king. 'I'll go now, and don't worry, we'll not come back to this place.' And he ran away from the moon lake as fast as his legs would carry him.

The hare smiled to himself and stirred up the water of the lake again with his paw. He watched the reflection of the moon dance and wriggle in the water. Then he called for the rest of the hares, to tell them that the elephant king had gone and would not be returning.

The barber who killed three monks   *Jumping to conclusions*
adapted from the Panchatantra Book Five

There was once a man for whom everything seemed to be going wrong. He lived in a tumble-down old house by himself; he had no job, he had lost all his money, his family had died, he had few friends, he was lonely, fed-up and depressed.

'What on earth is going to become of me?' he said to himself. As he sat by his miserable fireside staring into the flames, he began to see pictures – imaginary pictures in the heart of the fire itself. He could see people, faces, places. He grew drowsy and sleepy. His head nodded. And he dreamed.

He dreamed he saw three monks come into his room from the street outside. They spoke to him and said 'Tomorrow, when you are fully awake, we will come to see you again. We are not really three monks, but are three sacks of treasure in disguise. We were changed into monks many years ago by your great-great-grandfathers. It was done so that no-one could steal the gold. It was done to keep the gold safe until the day when someone in the family should really need it. We think that time has now come. This is what you must do. Tomorrow, when we come again, you must hit us quickly and hard. As soon as you do that we will change back into our original form – into three sacks of treasure. Do not be afraid of striking us, you will not hurt us. Goodbye until tomorrow.'

In the morning, when the man woke up, he could remember the dream quite clearly. He felt sure the three monks would come to his house, and he knew what he must do in order to turn them back into three sacks of gold.

He wanted to be ready for the visitors, so he cleaned the house from top to bottom. He gathered fresh flowers and put them on the table. Then he had a bath, put on clean clothes and called for the barber to come and trim his hair and his beard and his nails. He told the barber he was expecting special visitors.

'I can't pay you just yet, but I will be able to pay you soon,' he said to the barber.

Several minutes later there was a knock at the door.

'It'll be your visitors,' said the barber. 'I'll let them in.' He opened the door, but was astonished to see the man hit each monk hard as soon as he walked in.

The barber was then even more astounded to see each of the three monks suddenly change from a person into a bulging sack of treasure.

'This is worth remembering!' he said to himself.

The man then put his hand into one of the sacks, pulled out three hundred gold pieces, and gave them to the barber saying 'This is your fee. Now remember, don't say a word about this to anyone.'

'I won't, I won't,' said the barber.

And, in fact, the barber didn't say a word to anyone about the strange happenings in the man's house. But, a few days later, three monks called at the barber's house asking if he had anything to give to the poor, and he foolishly thought to himself, 'Well, now is my chance'. He hit each one of them as hard as he could, expecting them to turn immediately into three bags of gold, but couldn't understand it when they simply fell to the ground... dead. Neither could he understand it, when a little later, the police arrived and led him away charged with murder.

Later, when the man visited the barber in prison he said to him, 'It's a pity you didn't realise that when you don't see something properly, you don't understand it at all. Don't jump to conclusions next time'.

cf. 'Great Claus and Little Claus' by Hans Anderson, in which Great Claus is tricked into killing his horses and his grandmother by Little Claus. Great Claus jumps to conclusions based on what he sees, but not on understanding.

The mouse girl
What you look for may be under your nose
adapted from the Panchatantra Book Three

Once upon a time a clever man was swimming in the river, when a bird flew overhead and accidentally dropped a tiny mouse from its talons into the water.

'Poor thing. It'll drown,' said the man, and he scooped up the mouse in his hand, swam to the river's edge, climbed out, and carefully put the mouse on the leaf of a banyan tree. Then he went back to the water and finished his swim.

But as he swam he thought 'That was very cruel of me to leave the poor mouse all alone on the leaf of that tree. The poor thing must be cold and wet and shivering. She's escaped death by a whisker, first from a bird who would undoubtedly have eaten her, and second from drowning in the river. She's only a young mouse and she's been taken away from her mother and father and brothers and sisters and friends and home. I can't just leave her all by herself in the tree. After all, I rescued her, I am therefore responsible for her, I am her guardian; her adopted parent. I will go and rescue her again.

So the man once more climbed out of the water and went to the banyan tree. He gently picked up the tiny mouse, set her down on the ground, said some magic words – for he was a very clever man – and changed her from a mouse into a beautiful little girl.

'Come home and live with me,' he said. 'My wife and I will look after you and care for you as though you were our own daughter.'

'Thank you,' said the mouse-girl.

For several years the man and his wife and the mouse-girl lived happily and contentedly together. She was pleased to be their daughter and they were happy and proud to be her parents, for she was a lovely girl – kind, generous, cheerful, hard-working, dutiful, lively and bright.

As the mouse-girl grew older, the man began to think about her future.

'I want her to be happily married,' he said. 'I want her to have as happy a family as we have,' he said. 'I want her to have a good husband who will love her and care for her,' he said. 'I want her to have a husband who is strong and important and powerful. I want her to have a husband who is worthy of her.'

The man spent many days worrying about the future. He felt it was his job to find her a husband, and he worried about finding the right one.

'I know!' he said one day. 'I will ask the sun to be her husband. The sun is the strongest thing I know. Without him none of us would be here.'

So the man went to speak to the sun. 'I am looking for a husband for my daughter. You are strong and powerful. Will you marry her?'

'Nothing would please me more,' said the sun. 'But remember, the clouds are more powerful than I. They can cover me and make me invisible. Why not ask them?'

So the man went to speak to the clouds. 'I am looking for a husband for my daughter. You are strong and worthy of her. Will you be her husband?'

'We would love to,' said the clouds, 'But remember, the wind is stronger than we are. It can blow us in any direction it chooses. We are powerless to do anything but go where it commands. Why not ask the wind?'

The man went to speak to the wind. 'I am looking for a husband for my daughter; a husband who is strong and powerful and worthy of her. Will you marry her?'

'Gladly,' said the wind. 'But remember, the mountains are more powerful than I. It doesn't matter how hard I blow, I cannot move the mountains. They are stronger than me. Why not go and ask them?'

And so the man went to speak to the mountains. 'I am looking for a husband for my daughter. I know you are strong and powerful. Will you marry her?'

'With pleasure,' said the mountains. 'But remember, that although you think we are immovable, we are not. The mice are stronger than us. They constantly nibble holes in us. If you want a truly strong husband for your daughter, then go and ask a mouse!'

With that, the man went to the base of the mountain and asked to speak to a mouse. 'I have looked high and low for a strong husband for my daughter,' he said. 'And my search has led me to you. Will you marry her?'

'I cannot,' said the mouse. 'I would like to but I cannot, for she is human and I am a mouse. How could she come to live here in the mountain in my mouse house? It is impossible.'

'Oh no it's not,' said the man. And without further ado, he changed the girl into a mouse again – for he was a very clever man – and she went to live on the mountainside with the mice, and lived happily ever after.

cf. Aesop's 'The mouse' in which a female mouse seeks a strong husband. She asks to marry the wind but he refers her to a tower, The tower tells her it is being ruined by mice. The mouse realises she should marry her own kind since they appear to be the strongest creatures in the world.

The lion, his servants, and a camel   *Insincerity*
adapted from the Panchatantra Book One

A lion once lived in a forest with his three servants, a leopard, a jackal and a crow.

One day, as they were walking through the forest looking for food, they found a camel who had been accidentally left behind by some travellers.

'Whatever is it?' asked the lion, for he had never seen a camel before. 'It's a very strange looking creature.'

'Let's kill it and eat it,' said the leopard.

'Yes, let's have it for dinner,' said the jackal.

'And for tea and for breakfast as well,' said the crow. 'There's enough meat on it to last us for days.'

'No!' said the lion. 'Let's find out about it. What is it called and why is it here? Go and ask it.'

So the three servants did as the lion asked and went to speak to the camel. He told them he was a camel and that he had been left behind in the forest by the travellers.

The three servants went back to tell the lion what they'd found out.

'Let's let him live with us,' said the lion. 'He can't stay in the forest all alone;

anything might happen to him. He can stay with us and I will protect him. Bring him here.'

The leopard, jackal and crow went to tell the camel the news that the lion would protect him, and that he could live with the four of them. But the three servants were not happy with the arrangement. An extra animal meant an extra mouth to feed, an extra one to worry about, an extra friend to fit into the group.

Soon after the camel came to stay with the four animals, the lion became badly injured in a fight with an elephant. He limped back to his cave, crying with pain.

'I shall have to stay in here until I'm well again,' he said. 'You must go and find food for us all. I cannot hunt just now.'

The leopard, jackal and crow looked at each other. 'We can't leave you,' they said. 'We must stay here and look after you.'

'You will look after me better if you go and find us all something to eat,' said the lion. 'Go along. Bring back something tasty.'

The leopard, jackal and crow set off to hunt for food in the forest. But they found nothing. Not even a rabbit, or a pigeon, or a sparrow. Not even a grasshopper or a caterpillar.

'This is hopeless,' said the jackal. 'There's nothing here.'

'No,' said the crow. 'There's nothing here in the forest, but there's a camel back at the cave. We could eat him!'

'But the lion promised to protect him,' said the leopard. 'He'll never agree to eat him.'

'He will if we trick him into it,' said the crow. 'Listen!' And he whispered his plan to the jackal and the leopard.

The three animals went back to the cave.

'We're sorry,' said the jackal to the lion. 'But there's just nothing to eat out there. There's not a bird or an animal in sight. I'm afraid we're just going to have to starve to death.'

'Oh dear!' said the lion.

'Oh no!' said the leopard. 'We cannot allow you, our great and mighty lion, our protector, our guardian, to die. Oh no! I will save you,' he said.

'And how will you save me?' asked the lion.

'You can eat me,' said the leopard.

'But I couldn't do that,' said the lion. 'You have been my faithful servant all these years. I couldn't eat you.'

'Then you can eat me,' said the jackal.

'But I couldn't do that either,' said the lion. 'You have also been a faithful servant to me for many years. I couldn't eat you.'

'Then eat me,' said the crow.

'Don't be silly,' said the lion. 'I couldn't eat you. Anyway, you're far too small. I wouldn't dream of eating you.'

Now the camel had, of course, been listening to all this. 'It's quite clear', he said to himself 'that the lion isn't going to eat any of us. And he promised me his protection, so he won't eat me. Therefore I'll offer myself for him to eat, like the others have done.'

'You can eat me,' said the camel.

'You?' said the lion.

'Yes me,' said the camel.

'Right!' said the leopard.

'Yes!' said the jackal.

'Now!' said the crow.

And before the lion had time to think or blink, the leopard, jackal and crow seized the camel and killed him. Their plan had worked.

The sea and the sea-birds

Think before you speak or act/conceit

adapted from the Panchatantra Book One

Once upon a time a pair of sea-birds lived on the sea shore.

'Find me a place to lay my eggs,' said the female bird. 'It's time for us to have a family.'

'This place here is fine,' said the male bird. 'Let's stay here, you can lay your eggs in that scrape of sand at the bottom of the cliff.'

'I don't think it's safe enough,' said the female. 'What if there should be a high tide? The sea will sweep away the eggs and our babies will be lost.'

'The tide will not come up as far as this,' said the male bird. 'We'll be quite safe here.'

'Oh you will, will you?' said the sea, who had been listening to the birds' conversation. 'We'll soon see about that!'

The sea watched and waited. It watched the birds line the scrape of sand with a few sticks and bits of driftwood. It waited until the female bird had laid a clutch of six creamy white eggs in the scrape-nest. Then it heaved its waves together, swirled its surface into white foam, and swept up the beach, beyond the tide-mark, to the very base of the high cliffs. The two sea-birds took to the air in screaming terror, but the sea didn't care. It scooped up the six creamy white eggs in its waves and carried them away to its depths.

'Good!' it shouted. 'That'll teach them who's strongest.' And the sea laughed loud. But the sea didn't know what the birds would do.

At first the two sea-birds were too distraught and upset to do anything.

'I have never been so unhappy,' cried the female bird. 'My beautiful babies; my lovely eggs; destroyed.'

'I thought this place would be safe,' said the male bird. 'I didn't think that even the highest tide would reach up the beach as far as this.'

'What shall we do?' asked the female.

'We'll go and tell the other birds what has happened,' said the male.

He called a meeting of all the sea-birds and told them what the sea had done.

'We cannot fight the sea, he's too strong,' said the birds. 'But we can go and tell the king of the sea-birds what has happened. He will know what to do,' and they flew off together to tell him.

'I am so sorry to hear of your distress,' he said. 'And so sorry to hear that the sea picked a quarrel with you on purpose, and for no reason. There is no excuse for it. No excuse for one so strong and powerful to bully the weak and fragile. No excuse ever for deliberately causing hurt and unhappiness. But the sea shall pay for this. He shall be made to know that he has done wrong.'

'But what can you do?' said the birds. 'The sea is stronger than all of us. He will only laugh when we complain about his behaviour.'

'Yes,' said the sea-bird king. 'But he might not laugh so loudly if the great god Visnu speaks to him!'

And with that, the king of the sea-birds went to see the great god Visnu to tell him what the sea had done to the pair of sea-birds and their eggs.

When the god Visnu heard the story he looked serious. Then he smiled. Then he spoke in a thunderous voice to the sea, 'Give the sea-birds back their eggs, or I shall dry up your waves with tongues of fire and turn your waters to dry land!'

The sea felt suddenly afraid. Its bravado had gone. It stopped its gurgling laughter and calmed its foaming waves. Then it carefully lifted the six creamy white eggs from its depths, floated them to its surface and carried them on soft ripples to the base of the cliff, where it nudged them gently into the sand-scrape nest, whispering 'sssorry, ssso sssorry,' as it surged back to its bed.

'There! said the great god Visnu. 'I don't think you'll have any more trouble from the sea. I don't think he'll act again without thinking carefully first.'

The sea-birds thanked him for his help, thanked the rest of the birds for their help and understanding, and returned to the important business of hatching six creamy white eggs into fledglings.

cf. 'The Sea-bird's nest' page 93. Although the moral of the two stories is different, it is interesting to note the similarities in their beginnings.

See also 'The conceited sea' page 96, in which the boastful sea is also put in its place by a God.

Three fish   *Think for yourself*
adapted from the Panchatantra Book One

Once upon a time there were three fish who lived together in a large pool. Their names were Think-Ahead, Think-Now and Think-Not.

These may seem strange names for fish, but in fact they were very appropriate names, because the fish called Think-Ahead always did just that – he always thought and planned ahead. The fish called Think-Now never thought about was was going to happen, or indeed what had happened. He only ever thought about what was actually happening now. And the fish called Think-Not – well yes you've guessed – he simply didn't think at all, about anything, or anyone, ever.

One day the three fish were swimming around the pool as usual, when Think-Ahead saw some fishermen on the bank, and heard them talking.

'I think we'll come fishing here tomorrow. What do you think?' said one.

'Good idea!' said another. 'We've not fished here before.'

'Looks like a good place. There are plenty of fish in these waters,' said a third.

'Oh dear!' said Think-Ahead. 'That's the end of our peace and quiet in this pool. Never mind. I know a way through the stream to another pool, where we'll be safe. No fishermen go there. I'll tell the other two and we'll set off first thing in the morning before the men arrive.'

Think-Ahead swam up to Think-Now and Think-Not and told them what he'd heard and what his plans were. But, to his surprise, they didn't seem very enthusiastic.

'I'll worry about it when it happens,' said Think-Now. 'Anyway,' he added, 'they might change their minds and not come here after all, then we'll have changed pools for nothing. No; I'm stopping here for the time being.'

'And what about you?' said Think-Ahead to Think-Not.

'Mmm?' said Think-Not. 'What? Oh I don't know,' and he swam away after a tiny crab he'd just seen. 'Well, in that case I'm setting off now,' said Think-Ahead. 'I'm not waiting for tomorrow or for you two. Goodbye.' And he set off to find the stream that he knew would lead him to the safety of the other pool where fishermen never went.

Half way through the next morning the fishermen came to the pool. They threw huge nets into the water and scooped up in them anything that was there.

'Oh dear,' said Think-Now to himself. 'Think-Ahead was right. I wish I'd gone with him. Still, it's too late now. What can I do. Think. I know. I'll pretend I'm dead.' And Think-Now made himself quite still in the fishermen's nets. He didn't move a muscle. He didn't blink an eye. He didn't twitch or wriggle or cough or sneeze or even breathe. He lay perfectly still.

The other fish, Think-Not amongst them, were terrified to discover themselves caught in the nets and being pulled towards dry land. They thrashed about in the water; they tossed and turned, pitched and rolled and flung themselves about. But all to no avail. The nets were dragged out of the pool and onto the grass. Think-Now continued to lie still, wondering how much longer he could hold his breath.

'This one's dead!' shouted one of the fishermen, grabbing hold of Think-Now. He pulled him out of the heap of wriggling fish and threw him onto the grass.

Think-Now wasted no time. He flipped his tail as hard as he could and pushed himself back into the water. Then he swam for his life as fast as he could away from the nets, away from the men, away from the main part of the pool, and towards the stream that led to the other pool where fishermen never went.

'I wish I'd come here yesterday!' he said to Think-Ahead.

'I wish you'd both come here yesterday,' said Think-Ahead. 'So, what's happened to Think-Not?'

'I don't know,' said Think-Now.

They never did find out that Think-Not had no idea at all what to do when the nets pulled him to land. He just swam about, this way and that, until the men caught him... and killed him... and ate him.

The mongoose and the snake   *Jumping to conclusions*
adapted from the Panchatantra Book Five

There was once a man whose wife had just had a baby boy. He was a beautiful baby, and the man and his wife loved him very much.

When the baby was ten days old, his mother had to visit some friends and was unable to take the baby with her, so she left him in the charge of his father.

'Take good care of him,' she said. 'Look after him until I come home.'

'I will,' said the boy's father.

The man enjoyed talking to his son, and playing with him. He even read him a story, although of course the baby was too young to understand it properly.

But no sooner had he finished reading the story than there was a knock at the door, and one of the queen's servants stood there.

'Her Majesty says you are to come to the palace straight away,' said the servant. 'There is something she wants you to do. You must come now, immediately, with me.'

'But I can't,' said the man. 'I am looking after the baby. My wife has gone out and there is no-one else I can leave him with.'

'The queen will be angry if you don't come back with me straight away,' said the servant. 'She wants you to come now!'

The man stood and thought for a while. He couldn't just leave the baby on its own, but he couldn't take it with him to the queen's palace either. He wasn't sure exactly where his wife had gone, so he couldn't bring her back, and he dared not anger the queen.

'I know: I could leave my mongoose looking after the baby,' he said. Now the mongoose had been the man's pet for a long time. It was a lovely animal. It was kind and gentle, and it was always loyal and faithful. It was never in trouble, it never strayed far, and it always did exactly what the man told it to do.

The man quickly went back in the house, tucked up the baby in its cot, told the mongoose to sit next to the cot and guard the baby, then he set off with the servant to the queen's palace.

The mongoose sat quite still, but it was very alert. It knew it had been given an important job to do. It knew how much the man and his wife loved the new baby. It knew it must let no harm come to the baby. It concentrated hard on watching and listening.

For a long time the mongoose sat quite still. Then suddenly it turned its head. It had seen, or rather sensed, something move near the corner of the room. It stared at a small gap under the door. There... sliding... silently... soundlessly... stealthily... secretly... dangerously... was a snake. The mongoose froze. The snake crept closer and closer to the child's cot; its tongue tasting the air; its body curving and twisting towards the baby. The snake reached the edge of the cot and raised its head towards the sleeping child. The mongoose suddenly flew into action. It leapt on the snake, tipping the cot as it did so. Its teeth sank into the snake's neck and it shook it. Dead.

Just then, the mongoose heard the man opening the main door of the house. He was home again. The animal hurried out of the baby's room, hurried to try to tell the man what had happened. To try to explain how it had saved the baby. To try to say that it had been loyal and faithful to the man and his family. To try to show the man that his new baby was safe and that the snake was dead.

But the mongoose had chance to say nothing.

The man took one look at the bloodstains on its paws and mouth and decided for himself what had happened. He flew into the most terrible rage.

'How could you do this to me? How could you kill my baby? How could you? After all the care I have shown you all these years, and you repay me like this. Well, if you have killed my child, I shall kill you.' And without thinking any further, the man raised a stick to the mongoose and killed it.

Then, the man went to his baby son. He saw the cot overturned. He saw blood on the bedcovers. And he saw his baby lying on the floor. But he also saw that the baby was very much alive. It smiled and waved its arms at him. The man looked around the room, and saw a snake lying dead at the foot of the cot. Then he realised what a terrible mistake he'd made.

He sat in the room for a long time, after setting straight the cot and putting the baby safely inside again. Then he went to the mongoose and lifted its body gently in his arms.

'I'm sorry,' he whispered. 'I know now that you saved my son's life. I'm sorry I acted before thinking. And I'm sorry it's now too late to put things right.'

cf. 'Bedd Gelert' by William R. Spencer, in which a dog (Gelert), kills a wolf in his master Prince Llewellyn's absence. The master returns, sees blood on the dog's muzzle, assumes it has killed his child, and kills the dog, only to repent bitterly when he learns the truth. The story is also found in popular Welsh folklore, but with anonymous characters; and is found again in the Arabic 'Kalilah and Dimnah' where the mongoose is translated as a weasel.

See also 'The Bee-keeper and the bees' page 145. The theme of this Aesopian fable is the same as the above, although the story-line is different.

The crows and the snake

The strongest may not be the most clever

adapted from the Panchatantra Book One

Once upon a time there was a tall tree growing by the side of a lake, where a pair of crows and a cobra lived. The crows lived high in the branches of the tree and the cobra lived in a hole at the foot of the tree, amongst the gnarled roots. For a long time all went well; the crows didn't interfere in the cobra's life and the cobra took no notice of the crows.

Then the crows laid a clutch of eggs, and the cobra discovered it liked fledgling birds to eat. As soon as an egg hatched, the cobra climbed up the tree trunk, slithered along the branch, stole the baby bird, and ate it. The crows were powerless to do anything about it.

In despair they went to see their friend the jackal.

'Whatever are we to do?' they asked. 'Every time that cobra steals one of our fledglings, it is as if one of us has died, we feel so sad. Yet there seems to be nothing we can do. The cobra is so much more powerful than we are; we cannot fight him, or tell him to stop. We cannot make him leave our tree or stay at the bottom like he used to do. What shall we do?'

'It's a difficult question,' said the jackal. 'He is certainly much stronger and more powerful than you, so you must not even think of trying to fight him, for he will surely kill you. No: we must use our brains, for although we are not as big or as strong as the cobra, we can think just as well as him. What we need is a way of tricking him into leaving the tree, then you two can live in peace and bring up your family.'

The crows and the jackal thought and thought, but couldn't come up with a plan that might work. Then, as they were thinking, some girls came down to the edge of the lake to swim. They took off their gold bracelets and necklaces, their rings and their brooches. They put their jewelry on top of their piles of clothes and got into the water.

'That's it!' cried the jackal. 'I've had an idea that will make the cobra leave your tree!'

'What is it?' asked the crows.

'Listen carefully,' said the jackal. 'Fly down there to where the girls have left their jewelry. Make sure they see you flying around, then, when you're sure they're watching, steal one of the gold necklaces and fly off with it.'

'We can't do that!' said the crows. 'We can't take something that doesn't belong to us.'

'But you're not really going to *steal* it,' said the jackal. 'You're just going to borrow it! Now, listen to what you have to do next.' The crows listened and decided that the jackal's plan might work.

The female crow flew down to the jewels the girls had left, and, making sure they could see her, she picked up one of the gold necklaces in her beak. The girls saw what she did and began to shout and point. Then they came out of the water and chased her. They ran and called and jumped and shouted and tried to catch the crow, but she very cleverly kept always just out of reach, just a little in front of them, just a little above them, but never so far away that the girls might give up and go back to their swimming.

The crow led them, just as the jackal had advised, nearer and neared to the cobra's home at the base of the tree. The girls followed, all the time thinking that at any minute they would be able to catch the crow and get back their necklace.

Then, just as the crow reached the cobra's hole, she dropped the gold necklace. It landed right at the entrance to the hole. The girls arrived at the place, and the cobra came out of his hole to see what all the commotion was about.

'Ugh! A snake!' cried the girls. 'Get a stick and poke it out of the hole,' said one of them. 'Quick! Before it has chance to bite any of us,' said another. 'Kill it! Then we can get the necklace,' shouted a third.

The snake slid out of its hole and across the grass in an attempt to get away and save its skin. But, too late. The girls picked up sticks from the ground around the tree and hit the snake until it was dead.

Then the girls picked up their gold necklace and ran back to the lake to finish their swim.

'Well!' said the jackal. 'The plan worked, didn't it? The snake won't trouble you any more now!'

'No,' said the crows. But they had hoped that the snake would have been frightened away, instead of killed. They wanted him gone, but not dead.

However, they said thank you to the jackal and went back to their home in the treetop. There they raised a whole family of fledglings safely, and were never troubled by snakes again.

cf. 'The heron's revenge' in the Jataka Tales *(the Kuntani-Jataka). Whilst a heron is away from home delivering messages for the king, some boys come and squeeze her young to death. In revenge, the heron picks up the boys and drops them at the feet of a tiger who eats them.*

Further reading

For teachers
A Handbook of Hinduism for Teachers ed. by Dermot Killingley (Grevatt & Grevatt, 9 Rectory Drive, Newcastle-upon-Tyne NE1 4XF)
Comparative Religions ed. W. Owen Cole (Blandford Press 1982)
Indian Tales & Legends J.E.B. Gray (Oxford University Press)
Hindu Family in Britain P. Bridger (Pergamon Press)

Hindus and Hinduism Partha & Swasti Mitter (Wayland 1982)
Myths and Legends of India J.M. Macfie (T.& T. Clark)
Six Religions in the Twentieth Century W. Owen Cole with Peggy Morgan
   (Hulton Educational 1984)
Understanding your Hindu Neighbour J. Ewan (Lutterworth Press)

For children
Hindu Festivals Swasti Mitter (Wayland 1986)
Hindu Myths Wendy O'Flaherty (Penguin 1975)
Hindu Stories V.P. Kanitkar (Wayland 1986)
Hinduism – Dictionaries of World Religions Patricia Bahree (Batsford 1984)
Hinduism V.P. Kanitkar (Wayland 1986)
I am a Hindu Manju Aggarwal (Franklin Watts 1984)
Indian Mythology Veronica Irons (Hamlyn 1967)
Our Culture – Hindu (Franklin Watts 1988)
Stories from the Hindu World (Macdonald 1987)
The Hindu World Patricia Bahree (MacDonald 1982)

Useful addresses

Hindu Centre. 25 Hoop Lane, Golders Green, London NW11
India House. Aldwych. London WC2
Leeds University Hindu Society. Leeds University Union Leeds LS2 9NA
Royal Asiatic Society. 56 Queen Anne Street, London W1
Vedic Mission. 145 High Street, West Bromwich B70 6NY

Islam

Islam is the second largest world religion, with an estimated 800 million followers. Muslims are found in almost every country, although the majority live in the stretch of arid lands between Morocco and Pakistan. Indonesia has the largest single Muslim population, with over 100 million followers. Pakistan and Bangladesh also have a large Muslim population.

There are an estimated one million Muslims in Britain today, the majority of whom are from Pakistan and Bangladesh. It is believed that the first official delegation from the Muslim world came to London in 1394 CE at the invitation of Richard II, to give architectural advice on the building of Westminster Hall.

The numbers of Muslims in Britain remained low until recent times, but the building of the Woking Mosque in Surrey in 1889, indicated the growing number of British Muslims. Since then, commerce, trade and educational opportunities have contributed to the growth of Islam in Great Britain.

The Arabic word 'Islam' means submission, and Muslims – the followers of Islam – are those who submit to the will of God (Allah), and to the message of God as given to the Prophet Muhammad by the Angel Gabriel.

Muslims believe that Islam originated with the creation of man, and that Abraham, Noah, Moses and Jesus Christ are great prophets. But Muslims believe that the Prophet Muhammad is the last and greatest of the prophets.

Muhammad is believed to have been born in Mecca in 570 CE. As an adult he was concerned about the conditions and lifestyle of the people of Mecca. He spent much time in the mountains meditating, and it was there that he received his first revelation from God via the Angel Gabriel. This revelation called for Muhammad to denounce the paganism and polytheism of Mecca, and to teach that there is one God, Allah (meaning The God). Some of the people of Mecca became followers of Muhammad, but many turned against him.

In 622 CE Muhammad left Mecca to go and live in Medina at the invitation of its citizens. This departure (Hijra) marks the beginning of the Muslim calendar, because Muhammad established the first Muslim community at Medina. In 630

Muhammad defeated Mecca and rededicated the Ka'aba (a cube-shaped stone structure in the centre of Mecca) making it a shrine of pilgrimage for Muslims, which it remains to the present day. Muhammad died in 632 without naming a successor.

The revelations which the Prophet Muhammad received were assembled to form the Qur'an (meaning recitation). In about 650 CE the authorised version, written in classical Arabic, was prepared. Muslims believe the Qur'an to be the actual and final word of God. They regard it as the most important book in the world, which should be learned in its original Arabic and not in translation. Copies of the Qur'an are treated with the utmost respect.

The Qur'an is the focal point of Islam. It outlines rules of behaviour for the individual and for society, in addition to setting down historical facts.

The basic rules – the five pillars of the faith – are concerned with action as well as belief, and involve the individual interacting with others. The five pillars are:

1 *Shahadah:* the profession of faith, the belief that Allah is the one God.

2 *Salat:* the duty to pray five times each day. Before praying, a Muslim must wash. The prayers may be said in any clean place.

3 *Zakat:* the act of giving alms to help the needy and to support good causes, this should be done without advertisement.

4 *Saum:* the requirement to fast between dawn and dusk during the month of Ramadan.

5 *Hajj:* the obligation to make a pilgrimage to Mecca, at least once in a lifetime.

In addition, Muslims are obliged by their faith to be honest, fair and generous. They are forbidden to eat pork, drink alcohol, gamble or lend money for gain.

Islam has no tradition of fable as such, in its history. Its formal interpretation of the Qur'an excludes anthropomorphism. However, the Muslim world is rich with the heritage of ancient cultures of the Near East, and in folk-lore and legend. Muslim stories contain the essential Islamic characteristics of kindness, honesty, forgiveness, humility, devotion to Allah, and caring for all Allah's creatures.

The stories in this section of *Share our World* have been drawn from a variety of sources of Muslim folk tale and legend.

The two brothers   *Generosity/loyalty*
adapted from Islamic legend

Once upon a time there were two brothers who shared a farm. They shared all the work and they shared all the harvest. They shared everything equally... half and half... straight down the middle... fairly. They never argued or fell out about who should do what, or who should have what. They were always fair with each other.

One day, just after the two brothers had finished bringing in the harvest of corn, the younger brother said to himself 'My brother and I have equal shares of all the corn, but really he should have more than me. I live all alone and have only myself to look after, but he has a family, he has a wife and children to look after. He should have more than me, because he has more people to feed.'

But the younger brother knew that his older brother would never agree to take more than his half share of the harvest, so he thought of a plan.

That night, he went to his own store rooms, and he counted out six sacks of corn. He looked outside, to check that no-one was watching, and he carried the six sacks of corn to his brother's store rooms.

'There!' he said to himself. 'He will have extra corn, but I shall not tell him where it came from.'

Much later that same night, the older brother woke up suddenly from a dream about the harvest.

'I am really a very lucky man,' he thought. 'I have work to do each day and I have plenty of food. I have a wife and family to share it with, and I am very happy. But my poor younger brother has no family but me. I will give him some of my corn, to make up for not having a family. After all, he works just as hard as me, yet he is working only for one, so it is right that he should have extra.' And the older brother went to his store rooms, counted out six sacks of corn, and took them to his brother's store rooms.

'There!' he thought. 'But I shall not tell him it was me who gave him the extra corn.

In the morning, both brothers were astonished to find the same number of sacks in their store rooms, as had been there before they had each given six away.

'It's strange,' said the older one to himself. 'I'm sure I should have six sacks less!'

'This is odd,' said the younger one to himself. 'I gave six sacks away, yet I seem to have the same number that I started with.'

But neither brother wanted to tell the other what had happened, because neither wanted to show off about giving six sacks of corn away. So neither brother said anything at all.

The next year at harvest time the same thing happened again. Each brother secretly gave six sacks of corn to the other, and each brother could not understand why his store of sacks remained the same. But once more, the brothers said nothing to each other, because they did not want to show off about what they had done.

The following year, the same thing happened again... and again... and again. Every year the same. Every year a mystery. Every year six sacks gone, and six sacks reappeared. Every year six sacks given, and six sacks received. And every year neither brother knew how it had happened!

This story, identical except for the ending, is also found in Jewish folk-lore. In the Jewish version one brother decides to find out why his store of grain is not diminishing. He sees his brother giving up some of his harvest. Both brothers embrace, and King Solomon builds a temple on the place where the grain was given.

The ugly girl   *Goodness is beauty*
adapted from Islamic legend

Once upon a time a little girl was born to a family where there were already ten boys.

'A little girl at last,' said the mother. 'How happy I am.'

'A daughter for our family,' said the father. 'How wonderful.'

'A sister for us to care for,' said the sons. 'How pleased we are.'

'A baby girl,' said all their friends and neighbours. 'Congratulations.'

The new baby grew into a lovely child who was liked by everyone who met her. She was kind and gentle, unselfish and thoughtful to others. She always tried to do her best and always tried to be cheerful. But she was not a pretty child. In fact, some people were unkind and said she was ugly.

The girl's mother began to worry about her. She thought she might be upset at her appearance, so she removed all the mirrors from the house, and wouldn't allow any visitor to bring one in. And so the girl never saw herself, and didn't know what she looked like.

When the girl grew up, she met a rich and handsome man, who loved her for her kind and gentle ways, and wanted to marry her.

'Congratulations,' said everyone. 'We hope you'll both be very happy.'

But one girl, who was supposed to be her friend, felt jealous and angry, and said, 'Why should he want to marry you! You are ugly. Just go and look at yourself. I mean, have you ever seen such a face!' And she laughed cruelly at the ugly girl.

The girl began to cry, and went to find a mirror so that she could see for herself what she looked like, and whether she really was as ugly as her friend had said. But there was not a mirror to be found.

'Then I shall look in the lake at moonlight,' said the girl.

She waited until night, when the moon was high in the sky, and she went to the deep lake near her home. She took off her shoes and paddled into the edge of the water. She waited for the ripples to die away and the water to be still. Then she looked into the silver grey depths. She saw her reflection and saw that it was not beautiful.

'My friend is right,' she cried. 'How can anyone want to marry me, or even be my friend, when I look as ugly as I do. I must go away from here. I must go away from everywhere. I must go.' And the girl turned to run.

But there, standing behind her was another girl. A girl she had never seen before. A girl who was beautiful. A girl who was dressed in strange clothes, of a kind not worn in that part of the world.

'Who are you and why are you here?' asked the ugly girl.

'First, let me ask you a question,' said the stranger. 'Do you think that I am beautiful? Do you think that I am pretty?'

'Oh yes,' said the ugly girl. 'You are beautiful. You are so much more lovely than I am.'

'But I am you,' said the stranger. 'I am your good nature. I am what people see when they look at you. Oh not perhaps what strangers see; but I am what people see who know you. People who know you well, know how kind you are. They know how gentle you are, and how unselfish and caring you are. They know you are a good person, and they know what you are like inside. It is what is inside a person that matters. You could be the most beautiful girl alive, but if you were mean and nasty, cruel and unkind, that would make you ugly. You are not ugly, you are beautiful, because you are a good person. Now, no more running away. Go home and be happy.'

And the stranger walked away into the moonlit distance.

The girl who had once been ugly, went home, and in a little while was married to her rich and handsome man. They lived together in love and trust and friendship for the rest of their lives. For, to each other, they were both beautiful.

The woman and the cat
adapted from Islamic teaching

Caring for animals

There was once a woman who owned a cat. She was a large, untidy woman, with a frowning face and a cross expression. She never smiled and never had a good word to say to anyone, least of all her cat.

The cat was thin, with ragged, dirty, matted fur, and sore eyes and ears. It had once been a beautiful kitten, but was now starving and not far from death, because the woman didn't feed it properly, and didn't care for it.

One hot dry dusty day, the cat crawled out of the woman's dirty hut, and lay down in the shade of a tree outside. It couldn't get comfortable in the heat, and went back inside the hut. But she shouted at it and kicked it outdoors again.

Her neighbour saw what happened and called to her.

'How can you treat your cat like that? How can you be so cruel to a helpless animal? That cat is one of Allah's creatures; it's your job to care for it, to look after it. Look at it! The poor thing's starving.'

'Be quiet!' shouted the woman. 'It's nothing to do with you. It's my cat and I'll treat it how I want.' And she went back inside her hut.

The neighbour walked quietly towards the cat and spoke to it softly. The cat, at first, cringed away from him, but when it realised the man meant no harm, it allowed itself to be stroked, and then picked up and cradled gently into his arms.

'Come with me,' said the man. 'I'll not hurt you. Come with me and I'll give you something to eat.'

He took the cat into his house and set it gently on the floor. He gave it a dish of meat, and the cat ate greedily, unbelievingly, cautiously, in case the food should be suddenly taken away. But the food was not removed and the cat ate it all. It then moved a few steps away from the dish, sat on the floor and began to wash itself, purring as it did so.

But suddenly there was a shout from the door.

'I know you've got my cat in there. Give it back to me. You've stolen my cat. Bring it here. You've no right to have it here; it's not your cat. Give it back to me or I'll report you for theft.'

The man was unsure what to do. He didn't want to return the cat to the cruel woman, but he knew it was her cat. If he did not give it back to her, she could indeed report him for stealing it.

'If I give you back the cat, you must promise to care for it properly,' he said. 'You must feed it well and never hit it or kick it again.'

'I'll not hurt my little kitten-cat,' said the woman, in a silly, soft, wheedling sort of voice. 'Just give it to me!'

The man, reluctantly, handed over the cat. 'I'm sorry,' he said. 'I've got no choice. You belong to her.'

The cat struggled to get away from the woman, but she had tight hold of it. She carried it back to her hut and tied it with a piece of string to a chair.

'You'll not go out again and shame me,' she shouted. 'What I do with my own cat is my own business, and nothing to do with anyone else, do you hear?' and she kicked the cat under the chair.

The woman then ignored the cat. She didn't feed it or give it water. The cat grew thinner, and weaker, and eventually died. The woman threw it away.

The neighbour never saw the cat again after the woman had taken it from his house. He guessed what might have happened to it, but was unable to anything to help. After all, the cat belonged to the woman.

'But she was wrong to treat it as she did,' he said later. 'Every one of us has a duty to care for the animals that Allah has given to the world.'

The robber   *Forgiveness/greed/generosity*
adapted from Islamic legend

Once upon a time there lived a robber who was rich and famous. He didn't care who he stole from, or how much he upset people, as long as he got what he wanted. Many people asked him to stop stealing, and tried to make him live a better life, but he would not listen to any of them.

One night he broke into a house. He had no idea whose house it was, but it looked as though it might have valuable things inside it. However, when the robber climbed in through the window, he quickly saw that there was very little in the house worth stealing.

'What a waste of time and effort,' he said to himself. 'I wouldn't have bothered if I'd known there was nothing here worth taking.' But, having broken into the house, the robber was determined not to go away empty handed. There were several bundles of cloth lying around, so the robber decided to steal those.

He was just in the middle of tying them up, so that he could carry them more easily, when he heard a noise. He turned round and saw an elderly man standing behind him. The robber dropped the bundle of cloth he was holding, and started to run away.

'Just a minute,' said the old man, 'Don't go. I'll help you. There's too much here for you to carry all by yourself. Let's share the cloth between us. I'll carry half and you carry the other half.'

The robber decided that the older man must also be a thief, but he didn't see why they should have equal shares in the cloth, when he'd got there first.

'You can help me,' said the robber, 'but you can't have half the cloth. You can have a small amount, and I'll have the rest.'

'All right,' said the older man. 'Whatever you say,' and they both picked up some bundles and set off out of the house.

Soon the robber became impatient with the older man, because he couldn't run as fast and was struggling to keep up.

'Hurry up!' whispered the robber. 'If you don't move quicker than that, we're in danger of being caught. We've got to get to my hide-out before daylight. Come on! Be quick!'

The older man ran as fast as he could, but the bundles of cloth were heavy for him, and he was soon out of breath again.

'Come ON!' called the robber again, urgently, angrily. 'If I'd known you were going to be this slow, I'd never have let you help!'

At last they arrived at the robber's hide-out.

'Now, take those two bundles,' said the robber. 'You can have those for helping. Take them for yourself, and go. I don't want to see you again.'

The older man dropped the heavy bundles he had been carrying, and collapsed on to a chair.

'I don't want any cloth,' he said. 'I was just helping you. You see, it was my house that you broke into. It is my cloth that you took. You must be very poor to need it so badly. I thought the least I could do was to help you with it. And now that you know where I live, you can come and take anything, anytime, just whatever you want. You're very welcome to have what you want. Anything I have is yours.'

The robber could hardly believe his ears. He thought at first the older man was joking, that he was playing some sort of trick on him; but no, the man was perfectly serious.

'You are truly a good man,' said the robber. 'If I had not seen it with my own eyes, I would not believe what you did. First you let me steal from you, then you helped me carry your things to my house; you put up with my shouting at you, and now you offer to give me anything else of yours that I want. I cannot believe that you can be so good and kind after what I have done to you.'

'Perhaps you can learn something from what has happened,' said the older man.

'I am sorry for the life I have led,' said the robber. 'I am sorry for the upset and distress I have caused. I shall try to lead a better life in the future. Will you help me?'

'I will help you,' said the man.

cf. 'Les Miserables' by Victor Hugo, in which a bishop invites an ex-convict into his home to dine. The man steals silverware and is later caught by the police who return him to the bishop's house. The bishop denies that the man stole from him, and as added proof of this, hands him silver candlesticks which he says the man forgot. The criminal changes his lifestyle in response to the kindness he is shown.

See also 'Guru Nanak and the murderer' page 129, in which Guru Nanak makes a murderer change his ways by singing to him about God.

The boy who told the truth   *Honesty/forgiveness*
adapted from Islamic legend

A long time ago, there lived a boy who was very clever. There was no school in the village where he lived, so he begged his mother to let him go to the big school in Baghdad.

'It's a good school and it has good teachers,' he told his mother. 'If I went there I could learn many things. I could learn to read and write properly. I could learn about the world and about our people.'

'But Baghdad is a long way away,' said his mother. 'Where will you live when you get there? It is too far for you to come home every day.'

'I shall find somewhere to stay,' said the boy. 'But please let me go. I want to go to school.'

The boy's mother was not happy about letting him go so far from home, but she knew that it was unfair to make him stay in the village, where he couldn't go to school. So she said he could go, and bought him some new clothes and a bag of books.

Then she sewed some gold coins into the lining of his coat.

'Emergency money!' she said. 'If you have a problem, or a difficulty, or an emergency, then the money can be used. Otherwise, leave it where it is.' She gave the boy a basket of food for the journey, and a purse with some money for the journey.

'There!' she said. 'You're ready. Now remember, be good. And remember, always, always tell the truth. You can save yourself from a lot of trouble if you always tell the truth.'

The boy promised to remember what she had said, then he picked up his bags and set off.

The way from his home to the city of Baghdad was long and lonely. The boy was travelling in the days before cars and lorries, buses and trains. He was travelling in the days of unlit roads; in the days of danger from thieves and vagabonds; in the days of walking from one place to another.

He had not gone far on his journey when he heard shouting, and he turned to see a band of robbers running out of the hills towards him. He had no time to run away, or hide, so he stayed exactly where he was, in the middle of the path.

The robbers surrounded him. One of them pushed him and laughed in his face, 'And what have we here,' he said.

'I'm travelling to Baghdad,' said the boy. 'To go to school.'

'To go to school,' mimicked the robber.

'And what have you with you "to go to school"?' asked the robber, getting hold of the boy's bags and beginning to open them.

'I have books and clothes and food for the journey,' said the boy calmly. 'And some gold coins that my mother sewed into the lining of my coat.'

The robbers all stood still and stared. The boy must be foolish, they thought. People didn't usually tell them if they had any hidden money.

'You're lying!' said the chief robber.

'Indeed I am not,' said the boy indignantly. 'I am telling the truth. I have been told always to tell the truth.'

'But you would lie to us to save your money, wouldn't you!' said the robber.

'No I would not,' said the boy quietly. 'Telling the truth is more important to me than a few gold coins. Even if you threaten to kill me, I shall still tell the truth. An honest person tells the truth always, not just when it might help him to do so.'

The chief robber turned away and spoke to the others.

'This boy is not stupid, as we first thought. He is good. There are not many good people in the world. He doesn't deserve to be robbed. We will let him go, and take nothing from him.'

And so the boy was sent safely on his way. He heard later that the robbers had changed their wicked ways and had begun to lead good and honest lives, because of the example he had shown them.

The man who was rude
adapted from a Muslim legend   *Forgiveness/caring for others*

A teacher was once talking to a large group of people. They had invited the man to speak, and everyone was listening carefully – sometimes nodding their heads in agreement, or shaking their heads if they disagreed with something – but listening quietly and politely.

Everyone, that is, except one man, who was standing near the back of the group. He constantly interrupted and called out, he argued back and shouted. When he realised that the teacher was taking no notice of him, he shouted even louder and began to call the teacher names.

The other people in the group began to feel uncomfortable about the man's behaviour. Some people turned to him and said 'Be quiet!' or 'Sshhh,' or 'Stop shouting, we want to listen,' but the rude man took no notice and carried on calling out.

By this time, the things he was saying were really very offensive, very rude and very upsetting to the teacher, and the people began to look at one another with worried faces.

'What is he going to do about it?' they whispered.

'Will the teacher start shouting back at him?' they asked.

'Will there be an argument, or worse, a fight?' they wondered.

'He can't go on ignoring such dreadful behaviour,' they said. 'Surely he will do something to get his own back on such a rude man.'

But the teacher did nothing. He ignored the man's bad behaviour, and carried on speaking to the group. Eventually, the rude man stopped shouting, and went away.

When the teacher had finished talking to the people, he said goodbye and set off for home, but the man re-appeared and started to call him names again. The teacher took no notice and kept on walking. The man followed him, shouting at him all the way to the teacher's house.

When the teacher arrived at his front door, he turned to face the man.

'Would you like to come inside?' he asked politely. 'You can come for tea. I'll make some sandwiches and I've a new tin of biscuits we can open. You can share them with me. Then when we've had something to eat, we can sit down together and you can tell me all about why you're so angry with me. It'll be much more comfortable talking in my house, than trying to have a conversation out here in the middle of the street.'

The people who were nearby, were astonished to hear the teacher being so kind, so pleasant, so nice, to the man who had been so rude to him. They had expected there to be fierce argument at the very least.

The rude man was also surprised to be spoken to in a kind way, in a pleasant way, in a nice way, especially after the way he had behaved. He was so surprised in fact, that he forgot to be rude and objectionable any more, and said to the teacher, 'Well... yes please... I'd like to have tea with you.' And then he said 'I'm sorry I was so horrible to you. I know I was nasty and unkind. I am ashamed of my behaviour, and I won't do it again. I promise.'

And as far as anyone knew, he kept his promise, and tried always to be polite to people he met, and to be kind to them, and to treat them with honesty and respect.

Nasrudin's coat   *Jumping to conclusions/tolerance*
adapted from Muslim folk-lore

Nasrudin had lived in his village for a long time, and was well liked and much respected by the people. They would ask his advice, or go to him if they wanted to know something, and Nasrudin always did his best to help them.

One day a rich merchant who lived in a large house at the edge of the village, decided to hold a banquet. He invited all the villagers to the meal. It was to be a grand occasion.

'Are you going to the banquet, Nasrudin?' asked one of his neighbours.

'Of course I am,' answered Nasrudin. 'Everyone's going. Don't worry, I won't forget.' But Nasrudin did forget. He became so involved in working in his fields, that everything else went out of his head.

Much, much later, the neighbour came walking past. He was dressed in his best clothes and was on his way to the banquet.

'Hey, Nasrudin!' he called. 'What are you doing? You should be ready for the banquet by now. You surely haven't forgotten, have you?'

'Oh the banquet!' said Nasrudin as he remembered. 'I'll have to come as I am. I haven't time to go home and change, and if I'm late Rashid will think I'm very rude. I'm coming. Now. Straight away.' And Nasrudin, still in his working clothes, hurried out of his fields and along the road to Rashid's house.

When he arrived, he went in through the front door with lots of other guests, but he noticed that no-one spoke to him. In fact, it was as though people were deliberately ignoring him. People he had known all his life were turning away from him when he went near them. Even Rashid, who had invited him to the banquet, walked past him without speaking.

When it was time to sit down for the meal, things became even worse. There was not a place set for Nasrudin. There was nowhere for him to sit.

'But why?' said Nasrudin to himself. 'Why is everyone treating me like this? What have I done...' And then he looked down at his old, ragged, worn, dirty working clothes, and he thought he knew the answer.

Nasrudin left the dining room, and crept out of the back door of Rashid's house. He hurried to his own house and quickly changed into his best clothes. Then he went back to the banquet.

'Hello Nasrudin,' called Rashid, when he saw him. 'I'm so glad you could come. Come over here and sit down. There's a place next to me.'

'Hello Nasrudin', 'Nice to see you', 'Come and eat with us', called everyone else, as Nasrudin walked by.

Nasrudin went over to Rashid, who was holding out a chair at the place next to his. But Nasrudin didn't sit down. He stood behind the chair and took off his coat. He propped up the coat in the chair as though it was sitting at the table. Then he spoke to his coat.

'There!' he said. 'You sit in that chair and have a nice time at the banquet. I'll leave you now, but I'll come back later and collect you when it's time to go home,' and he turned to leave.

'Nasrudin?' said Rashid. 'Are you all right? Why are you talking to your coat? Why have you sat it at the table? Why are you leaving? Are you mad?'

'No,' said Nasrudin. 'But it is quite clear that you want my coat to come to your banquet, and not me. When I was in my old clothes, no-one wanted to speak to me, not even you, but now that I am wearing my best coat, everyone wants to be friends. So clearly it is my coat that has made the difference. In that case, my coat can come to your banquet, and I hope you enjoy its company!'

And with that, Nasrudin turned on his heels and left Rashid's house.

Stories of Nasrudin the mullah (teacher) are found throughout the Muslim world. Nasrudin is a popular folk-hero, often portrayed as foolish, but who nevertheless teaches a desirable code of conduct.

See also 'Nasrudin and the melon skins'.

Nasrudin and the melon skins   *Greed/tolerance/fair play*
adapted from Muslim folk-lore

There was once a man who was so wealthy he could afford the best house, the most beautiful clothes, the most expensive food, a whole army of servants, anything in fact that money could buy.

The man was a merchant, and had become rich by buying and selling all kinds of goods. Yet it never occurred to him to give away any of his wealth. He never thought of sharing any of his possessions or riches with others who were less fortunate than himself. It never crossed his mind to give up any of his time to help others, or to do any work to help other people.

The merchant was selfish, lazy and greedy.

The merchant knew everyone in the town where he lived, but of all the people he knew, the one he disliked the most was Nasrudin, the teacher. Nasrudin was fair and honest, kind and generous. Nasrudin knew that the merchant was lazy and greedy, and the merchant knew that he knew!

The merchant felt annoyed that Nasrudin thought him greedy and selfish, so he spent hours trying to work out a way of getting his own back. He plotted and planned to do something that would show Nasrudin up, make him look foolish in front of everyone, show him up to be not as good as everyone thought he was.

At last the merchant had an idea. This would teach Nasrudin a lesson. This would be a good trick that would make Nasrudin look silly in front of everyone.

The merchant invited Nasrudin, together with many important people of the town, to a meal at his house. He planned to serve melon for the first course. He made sure there were plenty of melons, so that the guests could eat as many as they wanted.

The guests arrived. The meal began. The melons were sweet, juicy and delicious. The guests ate a great many of them. Soon their plates were piled high with seeds and empty skins.

The merchant waited until he and Nasrudin both had lots of melon skins on each of their plates, then when Nasrudin wasn't looking, the merchant tipped all his empty skins on to Nasrudin's plate.

'Look!' he suddenly shouted, pointing to Nasrudin's plate. 'He talks to us about not being greedy! He teaches us that we shouldn't take more than our fair share, and just look at his plate. Look at what he's eaten. He's got twice as many melon skins as the rest of us. He's eaten twice as much as everyone else here. He's the greedy one!'

Everyone turned to look at the huge heap of melon skins in front of Nasrudin. 'It's true,' they said in disbelief. What a lot he has eaten. It is rather greedy to eat so many.'

The talking died down, and all the people looked at Nasrudin to hear what he would say.

Nasrudin looked at his own plate, now piled high with the melon skins. He looked at the merchant's plate, now completely empty with nothing on it at all, not even one tiny melon seed.

'Yes,' he said. 'It does seem greedy of me to have eaten so many melons. I do seem to have eaten more than anyone else here. But I am not the greediest one. Oh no! At least I ate only the juicy flesh from the middle of the fruit. There is someone here who was so greedy, they ate the flesh and the seeds *and* the skins as well. Look!' And Nasrudin pointed to the merchant's plate.

The merchant could think of nothing to say in his own defence. He had tried to trick Nasrudin, and failed. He felt ashamed, and promised himself to try to be fair to his neighbour in future.

See note at the end of the previous story.

Fair pay   *Greed/fair play/tolerance*
adapted from Muslim folk-lore

There was once a homeless man, who was wandering the streets having just spent his last coin. Now he had nothing. He had no idea where to go, or what to do. It was getting dark. Soon he would have to decide where to spend the night. Perhaps he would be able to find a doorway to sleep in, or a wall to shelter against. He hoped the night would stay dry and not too cold.

As he walked along, he suddenly became aware of a wonderful smell. The smell of meat and hot bread. The smell of gravy and vegetables. The smell of delicious, piping hot food. The man couldn't remember the last time he had eaten a really good, wholesome, solid, square meal. He followed his nose, turned the corner of the street, and came to a travelling food stall.

The stall was run by a large red-faced man in a big apron. He had a pot of soup simmering on a small stove, and a pan of stew bubbling on a hot-plate. There were rolls of bread toasting in a small oven, and vegetables in dishes on the counter. Hot steam was rising from the food stall, and all around it was the delicious smell of dinner.

There was a queue of people waiting to be served, and other people standing nearby, eating food they had just bought. It was obviously good food, judging by the way the people were enjoying it.

'I wish I could afford to buy some of that,' said the homeless man to himself. 'I've never smelled anything so good.' And he stood near to the stall so that he could carry on smelling the food.

'Hey! You!' shouted the stallholder to him. 'What do you think you're doing?'

The man, looking startled, turned round to see who the stallholder was shouting at.

'Yes, you!' called the stallholder. 'Come over here and pay me your money.'

'I'm sorry,' said the man. 'I think there must be some mistake. I'm not in the queue. I'm not waiting to be served. I haven't any money, so I can't buy anything.'

'Can't pay?' bellowed the stallholder. 'Then you're stealing. I'll have the police on you. Now come on, pay up. You're standing there smelling my food. I can see you smelling it. If you want to smell my food, you pay for it. So come on. Pay up.'

The man felt very afraid. He hadn't meant to steal the smell of the food. He didn't know he had to pay to smell it. And what if the stallholder should call the police. What would he do then. He'd never been in trouble before. What if they sent him to prison. The more he thought about all this, the more afraid and worried the man became.

Just then, a stranger stepped up to the stallholder.

'Do you think it's fair that this man should pay for the smell of your food?' he asked.

'I do!' said the stallholder. 'He can't have something for nothing. He has to pay.'

'Very well,' said the stranger. 'I will pay,' and he pulled out a purse full of coins.

The stallholder's eyes grew round with greed at the sight of the purse. But things didn't happen in quite the way he was expecting.

The stranger held out the purse and shook it hard. The coins inside jangled and rattled. 'Do you hear that?' asked the stranger. 'Do you hear the sound of the money?'

'Of course I can hear it,' said the stallholder. 'But I want to hold it, not hear it,' and he laughed.

'I'm afraid you won't be able to do that,' said the stranger, and he put the purse away again in his pocket. 'The sound of the money was your payment,' he said. 'That seems to me to be a fair price for the smell of your food.'

And everyone round about agreed with him.

cf. 'The boiled egg' page 89. In this Jewish tale, the same theme of just reward is explored.

The shopkeeper
adapted from Islamic legend   *Honesty/fair play*

There was once a man who had a shop. He sold cottons and threads, scissors and needles and pins and ribbons, and long lengths of material in every colour you could think of.

One day the man had to go out on business, to buy some new fabrics, and he left his assistant in charge.

'Look after the shop,' he said. 'And if anyone comes in and wants to buy that blue material, remember, you must sell it at half price. It's not perfect. It has a little dark mark in it, a flaw, that goes all the way along the length of cloth. So sell it for five pounds instead of ten.'

'I'll remember,' said the assistant.

He had a busy morning, after the shopkeeper had left. Someone wanted needles, someone else wanted scissors, a woman wanted some pale yellow satin, a man wanted a length of dark green cotton, then a customer came in wanting blue material.

'I'll know just what I want when I see it,' she said. 'What have you got in blue?'

The assistant showed her lots of different bolts of blue cloth. There was dark blue cotton and pale blue lace, deep blue silk and sky blue satin.

'No,' said the woman. 'Not like that. I need a blue that's like... that!' and she pointed to the length of blue cloth with the flaw. The length of blue material that wasn't perfect. The length of blue fabric that was half price.

The assistant reached down the cloth and spread it out on the counter for her to see. He knew he should say something about the flaw, but he didn't. He knew he should tell her that it wasn't perfect. But he said nothing. He knew he should say that the material was half-price because of the mark. But he didn't say anything.

'It's exactly what I want,' said the woman. 'How much is it?'

The assistant looked at the price ticket. It read ten pounds.

'Ten pounds,' he said. And he thought, 'If she's not even noticed the flaw, why should I tell her. If she's happy to pay ten pounds, why should I tell her it's only five. The shopkeeper will be pleased when he gets back. After all, I've made an extra five pounds profit for him!'

But the shopkeeper was not pleased with the assistant when he got back.

'It's dishonest,' he said. 'You knew that material had a flaw in it, yet you never said anything to her. You knew we should have charged her only five pounds, yet you charged her ten.'

'Well I don't know why you're complaining,' argued the assistant. 'You're five pounds better off than you would have been.'

'That's not the point,' said the shopkeeper. 'I'm going to find her. I'm going to give her the five pounds back.'

'You can't do that!' said his assistant. 'You don't know where she lives.'

'Then I'll find out,' said the shopkeeper, and that's exactly what he did.

When he discovered where the woman's house was, he knocked on the door, and then began to explain to her what had happened.

'But it's all right,' said the woman. 'I don't mind paying ten pounds. The material is just what I want. I know about the little mark, but it doesn't matter, I quite like it.'

'No,' said the shopkeeper. 'I want for my customers what I want for myself. I want you to be treated as I would want other people to treat me. I want to be honest with you because I'd like other people to be honest with me. So here is five pounds back,' and he handed the woman five pounds change.

'Thank you,' she said. 'I wish everyone in the world could be as honest as you.'

Further reading

For teachers
Approaches to Islam Richard Tames (John Murray 1982)
Comparative Religions ed. W. Owen Cole (Blandford Press 1982)
Fabled Cities, Princes and Jinn from Arab Myths and Legends Khairat Al-Saleh
   (Peter Lowe 1985)

Muslim Children's Library – a series of books for children of different ages. (The Islamic Foundation)

Six Religions in the Twentieth Century W. Owen Cole with Peggy Morgan (Hulton Educational 1984)

The Muslim Guide Mustafa Yusuf McDermott (The Islamic Foundation 1980)

The Religious Dimension; Islam Riadh El-Droubie and Edward Hulmes (Longmans 1980)

Stories of the prophets of Islam in 10 volumes (Macmillan 1985)

For children

Celebrations – Muslim Festivals Jane Cooper (Wayland 1989)

I am a Muslim Manju Aggarwal (Franklin Watts 1984)

Our Culture – Muslim Jenny Wood (Franklin Watts 1988)

Our Muslim Friends Anne Farncombe (National Christian Education Council 1977)

Stories from the Muslim World Huda Khattab (Macdonald 1987)

The Muslim World Richard Tames (Macdonald 1982)

Useful addresses

Islamic Arts Foundation. 5 Bathurst Street, London W8
Islamic Book Centre. 120 Drummond Street, London NW1
Islamic Foundation. 223 London Road, Stoneygate, Leicester LE2 1ZE
Muslim Educational Trust. 130 Stroud Green Road. London N4 3RZ
Muslim Information Service. 233 Seven Sisters Road, London N4 2DA
UK Islamic Mission. 148 Liverpool Road, London N1

Judaism

The history of Judaism stretches back 3500 years. It is the world's second oldest major religion, and together with Hinduism pre-dates people's ability to write. Judaism is the oldest of the three great monotheistic religions, and is the foundation of both Christianity and Islam.

There are believed to be almost 15 million Jews in the world today, of whom approximately a quarter live in Israel. The USA has the largest Jewish population with an estimated 5.8 million people. About 1.8 million Jews live in Eastern bloc countries, and an estimated 400,000 Jewish people live in Britain. Some two-thirds of British Jews live in London. The first Jews came to England in the eleventh century, but were expelled in 1290. It is believed that Jews did not return to England until the mid 17th century.

In the years between 1800 and 1940, there was a large increase in the world Jewish population, especially in Eastern Europe. During the Second World War, centuries of Jewish persecution culminated in the murder of six million Jewish people, in what was to become known as the Holocaust. Despite there being relatively few Jews left in the countries of Eastern Europe, anti-semitism still continues.

The early history of the Jewish people is told in the Bible: the Exodus from Egypt, the settlement in the Land of Israel. But independence was not to be Israel's for long. Foreign nations conquered the land and the Jews, deprived of their homeland, wandered to whichever countries would receive them. Throughout their wanderings they preserved their racial, cultural, religious and traditional identity.

In 1948 the State of Israel was established, helped by Jews world-wide, and especially by those of the USA. (America and France were the first two countries to recognise Jews as equal citizens – in 1783 and 1791 respectively.)

Judaism teaches that there is one God: all-knowing, eternal, the creator and ruler of the universe. God revealed the Torah (the Pentateuch, or first five books of the Bible), to the Israelites, and led them into the Holy Land. The Torah is accepted as the Law of God, and the people of Israel as the chosen people, because it was to them that God revealed the Law.

Obedience to the Law is central to Judaism. The 613 commandments within the Torah are believed to be the expression of God's will. Jews believe they have a duty, both to God and to humankind, to live in accordance with God's will. Jews believe that all are created equal, that all should be respected, that the under-privileged should be cared for, as should the environment. They believe that humankind is created with the free will to choose between good and evil, that the world we are given is good and bountiful, and that it is our duty to use it well, for the sake of humanity and in the service of God.

Maimonides – a Rabbi and great philosopher of the 12th century – drew up the Thirteen Principles of the Faith. He saw 'right belief' as being of great importance, and although Maimonides' analysis has been subsequently criticised by scholars, it is generally considered to summarise the essentials of Jewish belief. The Principles are

1 God is the creator of everything
2 God is one
3 God is spirit and not flesh
4 God is eternal
5 God alone is to be worshipped
6 God communicates to man through the prophets
7 Moses was the greatest of the prophets
8 The Torah (Pentateuch – the first five books of the Bible) was revealed to Moses at Sinai
9 The Torah, or Law, will not be changed
10 God is all-knowing
11 God rewards or punishes people for their good or evil deeds
12 The Messiah will come
13 The dead will be resurrected

Jewish traditional and folk literature provides rich and colourful tales, legends, fables and parables, drawn from different times, reflecting the historical experiences of three thousand years of Judaism, and showing the influence of other nations where the Jewish people have lived. The stories reflect the richness and variety of Jewish culture itself, and the literature has become an integral part of the Jewish heritage.

Jewish stories, though varied, have certain unifying characteristics. They celebrate wisdom and piety, and use humour and wit to provoke thought. The first story-tellers rarely missed an opportunity to point a moral lesson, and to inspire in their listeners a pride in their people and a trust in God.

King Solomon and the bee

adapted from Jewish legend

Loyalty/keeping your word/
small can be powerful

King Solomon was once sitting in his throne room, talking to his ministers, when a small bee flew into the room.

'Quickly!' shouted the ministers, 'Catch it, before it has chance to sting the King.' And the ministers began to jump and dance around the room in an attempt to catch the tiny bee.

But King Solomon, who was very wise, knew that the bee would not sting him, unless he did something to frighten or endanger it, so he sat very still and waited for the bee to fly near to him. When it did, King Solomon gently caught it in his hand.

'Oh please don't kill me,' said the small bee. 'Please let me go. If you spare my life now, I might be able to help you at some time in the future.'

The king laughed. 'You?' he said. 'Help me? The cheek of it! How do you think you, such a tiny little thing, could ever help me, a great and powerful king? But I'm not going to harm you. I'm going to let you go, just for your impudence!' And King Solomon walked to the window and released the little bee into the air. Then he forgot all about the incident.

Several weeks later, the Queen of Sheba came to visit the king. The Queen of Sheba had heard how wise King Solomon was, and she was determined to find out for herself if it was true. She was sure that he couldn't be as clever as everyone said he was, so she had devised all kinds of tricks and riddles to try to catch him out, and show him up in front of all his people.

She brought him a gift of a beautiful diamond. In its centre was a twisting hole. 'Thread it for me, like a needle,' she said. She was sure that the king wouldn't be able to do it. But King Solomon sent for a silkworm, and set it down at the edge of the diamond. The silkworm wriggled and twisted its way through the hole, drawing its silken thread behind it.

'There!' said the king, holding up the diamond, which spun and sparkled on the end of the thread.

The queen felt cross.

The next day, the Queen of Sheba arranged for one hundred little girls and boys to come before the king. They were all exactly the same age, exactly the same size, and dressed exactly alike in identical clothes.

'Now!' she said. 'Sit there and tell me which are boys and which are girls.'

King Solomon looked at the children. Then he sent for a servant. 'Bring me one hundred bowls of water, one hundred bars of soap and one hundred towels,' he said. He ordered his servants to give out the things, then 'Wash!' he said.

The boys dived in to the bowls of water, and the girls dabbled daintily! (Girls did that in those days!) King Solomon was easily able to tell the Queen of Sheba, which children were which.

The queen felt angry.

The next day, the Queen of Sheba ordered the royal florists to make 499 artificial roses. She ordered that each one must look like, and smell like, and feel like, a real rose. Then she went out into the royal garden and picked a single real rose. She hid it amongst the artificial roses, and asked King Solomon to pick out the real one.

King Solomon thought the task would be easy. But the more he looked at the flowers, the more he realised that he could not tell them apart. The artificial ones were so life-like. He could not find the real rose by looking; he couldn't tell which was the real rose by smelling; and even when he touched the flowers, they all seemed to be the same.

'She has beaten me,' he thought. 'She has found something which I cannot do. And now all my people will know that I am not as wise as they think I am.'

King Solomon was just about to admit defeat to the Queen of Sheba, when he heard a small buzzing sound by his ear. It was a tiny bee.

'Leave it to me,' said the bee. 'I will go deep inside each flower. I will find the real one, because that one will have nectar inside it.'

The tiny bee, unnoticed by everyone else in the room, flew between the petals. It dipped in and out of each flower and soon found the nectar. It hovered over the real flower, and when it was sure the king understood which was the true rose, it flew away towards the window.

The king slowly picked up the rose from the garden, 'This is the flower you are looking for,' he said to the Queen of Sheba as he handed it to her.

The queen felt furious.

The king turned to the window and whispered to the tiny bee, 'Thank you. I'm sorry I said you were too small ever to be able to help me. I was wrong. No-one is so big and powerful that they never need help, and no-one is too small that they cannot give help. I will never again judge someone's usefulness by their size.'

cf. Aesop's 'The lion and the mouse', in which a lion agrees to release a mouse but scorns its offer of help in return. The mouse later saves the lion's life by gnawing through netting in which the lion is caught.

cf. 'Androcles and the lion', a Christian legend in which Androcles removes a thorn from a lion's paw. Androcles is later condemned to death for his Christian beliefs, is put in a lion's den, but is saved by meeting the same lion he helped earlier, who refuses to harm him

The man and the pomegranate seed   *Honesty/fair play/tolerance*
adapted from Jewish folk tale

There was once a man, who through no fault of his own had become very poor. He was a hardworking man, but at that time, he had no job. Gradually he had sold all his possessions to raise money to buy food, but at last the day came when he had nothing left to sell. The man walked into town to look for work again. He was prepared to do anything, any job that anyone wanted doing. But there was no work to be had.

The man walked along the streets feeling depressed and dejected. He passed a shop selling meat pies, The smell of them made him feel hungry, but he knew he couldn't afford to buy one.

'Then I'll steal one,' he said. And before he really thought about what he was doing, he was inside the shop, grabbing a pie from the counter, cramming it into his mouth, and running away again as fast as his legs would carry him.

But it was not fast enough. He was caught and taken before the king.

'This is a serious business,' said the king.

'I've never ever stolen anything before,' said the man. 'I'm really sorry. I didn't mean to do it. But I was so hungry and I didn't have any money to buy any food. I'll never do it again,'

'No, you won't!' said the king. 'Because I am going to sentence you to death. You will die tomorrow. Take him away,' he said to the guards.

'Please sir,' said the man. 'Before I die, I want to show you something. I have a pomegranate seed. Look!' and he took out of his pocket a small seed.

'And why would I want to look at a silly seed?' asked the king.

'Because it's a magic seed,' said the man.

The king became interested.

'And what does this magic seed do?' he asked.

'As soon as it is planted, it grows before your very eyes,' said the man. 'You can watch its leaves growing and its flowers forming. You can see the pomegranates swelling and ripening. It only takes two minutes from planting the seed, to picking a pomegranate. You could be eating a ripe juicy one, two minutes from now.'

The king was intrigued.

'But if it's as magic as you say, why haven't you planted the seed?' he said.

'Ah, well, that's the problem,' said the man. 'It only works if it's planted by someone who has never stolen anything, ever, in their whole life. So you see, it wouldn't work for me, would it?'

'No,' said the king. 'It wouldn't work for you.'

'So, you have it,' said the man, and he handed the king the small seed.

'Er, I'm not sure. You have it,' said the king to his minister, and he handed the small seed on.

'Oh no,' said the minister. 'I don't want it. You have it,' he said to the guard.

'Not me,' said the guard. 'I don't want to plant it. You take it back,' and he gave the small seed back to the king.

'Oh dear!' said the king, and he looked most unhappy and uncomfortable.

'No-one seems to want to plant my magic pomegranate seed, do they?' said the man.

'Well, no,' said the king. 'You see, when I was a little boy, I once took one of my father's jewels without asking. There was a terrible to-do about it, but I never owned up. So you see, I am not able to plant the seed either.'

'And I,' said the minister 'I once deliberately gave someone the wrong change from some taxes they were paying me. So I can't plant the magic seed.'

'I can't plant it either,' said the guard. 'I once borrowed a beautiful pair of boots, from a friend. But when it was time to give them back, I said I'd lost them, so that I could keep them.'

'It seems to me,' said the man, 'that there aren't very many of us who are completely honest. And it also seems to me unfair: I stole because I was hungry and I am to be punished for it with my life, and yet you – who stole for greed – have had no punishment at all.'

'You are right,' said the king. 'You can go free. I take back the order to have you killed. I am sorry I gave you such a harsh punishment, and I am sorry for being less than honest in the past. I should not have criticised you, for something I have also done.'

The man put the small seed back in his pocket, and left the king's palace.

The boiled egg   *Greed/fair play*
adapted from a Jewish legend

Once upon a time an army was resting after fighting, and all the soldiers were given boiled eggs for supper. One of the soldiers, Adam, was very hungry and quickly ate his meal, but when he looked around and saw everyone else still eating, he realised his hunger had not gone away.

The soldier turned to his neighbour, 'Joshua, will you give me one of your eggs?' he asked. 'I'm really hungry.'

I'll *lend* you one,' said Joshua. 'But one of these days, when I want you to repay me the egg, I shall expect you to.'

Adam was somewhat surprised to hear to hear that Joshua might want the egg back one day, but he was so hungry that he agreed to repay the loan whenever Joshua wanted him to. Then he forgot all about it.

Six years went by, and the two soldiers remained in the army, but no further mention was ever made of the boiled egg. Then, one day, quite unexpectedly, Joshua went to speak to Adam.

'About the loan of the egg,' he said.

'Egg?' said Adam.

'Egg!' said Joshua. 'Don't pretend you've forgotten about it, because I know you haven't. I've come for the repayment of it today. Now, I've worked it out that you owe me about six million pounds.'

'Six million pounds!' exclaimed Adam. 'Don't be silly. I can't possibly owe you six million pounds for one boiled egg. Anyway, I haven't got six million pounds.'

'You owe me six million pounds,' repeated Joshua. And I want the payment now.'

Adam realised that Joshua was not joking. He was being perfectly serious.

'But how can I possibly owe you all that?' he asked.

'I lent you an egg six years ago,' said Joshua. 'That egg in the first year would have grown into a hen. In the second year, that hen would have had 20 chickens. In the third year the 20 chickens would each have had 20 more. In the fourth year there would have been 8000 chickens; in the fifth year there would have been 160,000 chickens; and this year there would have been over three million chickens from my one egg. Chickens cost about two pounds each, therefore you owe me just over six million pounds.' And he held out his hand for the payment.

Adam didn't know what to do. After all, he had agreed to pay back Joshua for the loan of the egg, but he never ever thought he would be asked to pay back over six million pounds. He didn't have six million pounds. He would never have six million pounds as long as he lived.

'You'll have to give me time,' he said. 'You'll have to give me time to sort out how to pay you,' and Adam dejectedly walked away, knowing that he would never be able to repay the debt, no matter how long he lived or how hard he worked.

But just as Adam was walking away, Solomon – the king's son – came striding by.

'You don't look very happy. What's the matter?' he asked. Adam explained the problem.

'Listen,' said Solomon, and he whispered something in Adam's ear. His face suddenly brightened, he said thank you to Solomon, then hurried away to a nearby field.

Adam set to and ploughed the field, then he lit a small fire, boiled a pan of beans, and started to plant the hot beans in the ploughed field.

By now a small crowd had gathered to watch Adam doing these strange things. Joshua joined the crowd.

'What's going on?' he asked.

'This stupid man is planting boiled beans,' said one of the crowd. 'He must be mad if he thinks boiled beans are going to grow.'

'Hey, what do you think you're doing?' shouted Joshua to Adam.

'I'm doing it for you,' Adam called back. 'All the money I get from these beans when they grow, is for you, to pay off what I owe you.'

'You idiot!' shouted Joshua. 'Those beans will never grow. You can't grow plants from beans that have boiled.'

'Oh yes I can,' said Adam. 'If your boiled egg could have grown into live chickens, then my boiled beans can grow into plants,' and he carried on working in the field.

Joshua knew he was beaten. He knew that his trick to fool Adam into paying him large sums of money as repayment for the egg loan, hadn't worked. Joshua hung his head in shame, and walked away from Adam and the field of boiled beans.

'I suppose if a boiled egg is borrowed, then a boiled egg should be returned,' he said to himself. 'It wasn't honest to try to get more from Adam than that.'

But Joshua never again suggested that Adam repay him the loan of the egg.

cf. 'Fair pay', page 80. Both stories have the same theme of fair reward for greed.

The fox and the grapes
adapted from Jewish folk-lore

Greed/think before you act

One day a hungry fox walked past a vineyard. He saw the rows and rows of neat vines, each carrying large bunches of fat, ripe, juicy, dark, purple grapes. The fox's mouth watered at the sight of all that fruit. 'If only I could get at it,' he thought. For, although the fox could see the grapes, he had no means of reaching them because the vineyard had a stout wooden fence all the way round it.

It was one of those fences that had strong square upright posts every so often, and long horizontal bars stretched between them. Wooden palings were nailed to the bars, very close together, with just a tiny carefully measured gap between each one. A tiny gap just wide enough for a fox to poke his nose in, but not wide enough for a fox to squeeze his body through.

The fox paced along the length of the fence. He found the gates – locked. He wondered about trying to jump over the fence and had one or two tries, but he knew it was too high, too tall, too big for him to leap over. Then he found the loose piece of wood. It was still fastened at the top, but it had become loose at the bottom. When he poked his nose into the gap between it and the next paling, it moved aside, leaving a small triangular shaped space.

The fox nosed into the gap. He pushed his head into the space. He nudged his shoulders into the opening. And then he stuck. Fast. He was just too big to fit.

In panic he wriggled free and shook himself. Then he tried again. It was the same. Again and again he tried to squeeze himself into the gap, which he knew was too small, but he was determined to reach those delicious grapes.

'If only I was smaller, thinner, skinnier,' he said. And that gave him the idea.

'If I stay here for a couple of days, and eat nothing and drink nothing, I shall be thinner. Then I'll be able to get in through the gap.'

So the fox waited, all day, all that night, all the following day and night, and in that time, he ate nothing and drank nothing. He lay on the dusty road, guarding his gap, only moving if he saw something or someone coming, when he slunk away so as not to be seen.

Every so often he tried the gap for size again. But even after two whole days, he still could not fit through. 'Another day and night,' he said. 'Then I'll be able to get in.' By now he was weak with hunger and thirst. But still he wouldn't give up.

At the end of the third day of waiting he tried once more. First his nose, then his head (OK so far), then his shoulders (he had to wriggle and turn, but they slid into the gap), then his front paws (over the wooden bar at the base of the fence), then a squeeze for his body, now his hips (another wriggle), then his back legs (step over the bar), and lastly a whisk with his tail... and he was IN.

He ran to the first bunch of grapes and devoured them in a single swallow. On to the next bunch and the next. Never had he tasted anything so delicious, so refreshing, so nutritious. The grapes dealt with his hunger and thirst all at the same time. He lay on the ground under the grapes and ate until he could eat no more. The juice ran down his chin and soaked into his fur. Then he slept.

He awoke when the moon was high overhead and shining brightly. He knew he must go now, he had stayed too long as it was. Someone might come and discover him. He knew what farmers did to foxes they found on their land.

He ran to the gap in the fence and pushed his nose through. The loose paling moved aside. He pushed his head through, and his shoulders. But there he stuck. After all those grapes he was no longer the starving, skinny, bag of bones he had been a few hours earlier, when he had squeezed his way into the vineyard.

The fox knew there was only one thing to do. He found the safest place he could to hide in, then he waited... one day... two days... three whole days and nights... without a single grape, until he grew thin and hungry again. Only then could he escape from the vineyard.

'I was hungry when I came in,' he said. 'And now I am hungry when I leave. I wonder if it was all worth it?'

cf. Aesop's 'The greedy fox' in which a fox climbs into a hollow tree trunk and steals food which shepherds have left for their dinners. The fox eats all the food and becomes so fat that he cannot get out of the tree. He calls to his friends to help, but the only advice they can offer, is that he must wait to grow thin again before he can escape.

The sea-bird's nest
adapted from Jewish fable   *Revenge*

There was once a bird who decided to build her nest close to the sea. She searched for the ideal place and eventually found a smooth ledge near the bottom of a cliff.

'Just right,' she said. 'The nest will be safe and sheltered here.'

The bird gathered twigs and straw, leaves and moss, and wove them all together to make a perfect nest. Then she sat back to rest.

But, while she had been nest-building, the sea had been slowly, silently, gradually, creeping up the beach. It stretched out its foam-edged waves towards the base of the cliff, then lifted itself towards the smooth ledge on which the nest was built. It licked at the edge of the nest, then lapped against it. Then the sea washed over the ledge and swept the nest away.

The bird flew up into the air, screaming and flapping her wings. She watched in dismay as her nest disintegrated in the swirling waters. The twigs and straw, leaves and moss floated for a while on the sea, then sank underneath the waves.

'How dare you?' called the bird. 'How dare you destroy my nest? Didn't you see me building it? Didn't you see how much time and effort it took me?' But no matter how much the bird shouted and questioned, the sea made no reply. It continued to surge against the cliffs until it was time for it to turn and make its journey back down the beach to the low water mark.

'Well, I'll get my own back on you,' shouted the bird. 'I'll get my revenge. I will destroy you just as you destroyed my nest. I'll empty you of all your water and then you'll be all dried up and useless. I'll destroy you and then you will never be able to spoil anyone's nest again.'

The bird swooped down to the sea and scooped up a few drops of water in her beak. She flew up to the cliff top and spat out the water on the grass. Then back to the sea for another beakful of water and up to the cliff top to empty it out. Over and over again she did this, in the belief that she was emptying the sea.

Soon she was exhausted, but still she kept on going, because she was determined to get her revenge on the sea. She didn't seem to notice that no matter how many beakfuls of water she took from the sea, it never became any smaller. The water still surged as high, the waves still beat as strongly and the tide still swept across the beach.

The bird, exhausted almost to the point of death, rested for a few moments on a rock, and was joined by another bird.

'I've been watching you,' said the newcomer. 'I can see what you're trying to do. But, may I give you a piece of advice?'

The tired bird had not the strength to answer.

'Revenge is a poor master,' went on the newly arrived bird. 'Getting your own back doesn't do any good. I mean, look at you. You are nearly dead with exhaustion, and what good has it done? The sea is as strong as it was before. It hasn't even missed the few drops of water you have managed to take away. You will not beat the sea, it's too strong, too powerful, too mighty, too great. You'd do better to save your energy and use it to do something useful. Think about it!' and the second bird flew off.

The exhausted bird did nothing for a long time. She didn't try to remove any more water from the sea, she didn't move. She sat on the rock where she was resting, and thought.

Some time later, she shook herself, fluffed up her feathers, preened herself a little, then flew to the top of the cliff.

She searched for the ideal place to build a nest and eventually found a smooth ledge near the top of the cliff.

'Just right,' she said. 'The nest will be safe and sheltered here.'

She gathered together twigs and straw, leaves and moss, and wove them all together to make a perfect nest. Then she sat back to rest.

'It's better to use my energy to do something useful', she said, instead of wasting it in trying to get my own back on the sea. Revenge is a poor master.'

cf 'The sea and the sea-birds' on page 59. Although the moral of the two stories is different, it is interesting to note the similarities in their beginnings.

Chicken soup   *Greed/selfishness*
adapted from Jewish folk-lore

There was once an old woman who lived all alone. One day she stood in her kitchen and wondered what to make for her dinner.

'I think I'll have some chicken soup,' she decided. So she gathered together the ingredients for her soup – some carrots and barley, a few leeks and onions, some peas and some parsley, a handful of herbs, a pinch of pepper and a shake of salt, and a fine, fat chicken. She put all the ingredients together in a large pan, added water, and set the pan on the stove.

Soon it was boiling and she turned down the heat so that the soup would simmer. The old woman simmered the soup for one hour, for two hours, then for half an hour more. Then she looked at it and tasted it.

'Delicious!' she said. 'I'll just put in some little light dumplings, let it cook for another half hour, and then it will be ready.'

Meanwhile, her next-door-neighbour was looking in *her* kitchen to see what *she* could have for dinner. She opened her cupboard. Nothing! She looked in the pantry. Empty! Even the last of the flour was used up. But as she searched for something to eat, her nostrils twitched. She could smell chicken... cooked chicken... hot chicken... chicken with herbs and dumplings... chicken smells, which unless she was very much mistaken, were coming from next door.

'I'll pop round,' she said to herself. 'Surely my neighbour will share her dinner with me, when she knows that I've got nothing to eat.'

She hurried next door, and knocked, just as the old woman was lifting the pan off the stove, ready to serve out the soup. She banged the lid back on the pan, and went to answer the door.

'Hello,' said her neighbour. 'I can smell your dinner cooking. It smells delicious. I've got nothing to eat in my house. Could I please share some of your dinner?'

The old woman thought of her lovely soup, hot and steamy and ready to eat. But she couldn't bear the thought of sharing it. Not even with someone who had nothing to eat.

'Dinner?' she said to her neighbour. 'No, I'm not cooking dinner. It must be someone else's dinner you can smell.'

'No,' laughed the neighbour. 'It's yours. I can smell chicken cooking. Anyway, I can see the pan on the stove.'

'Pan?' said the old woman, as though she had never heard of a pan before. 'Oh, pan! No, that's not my dinner cooking. That's, er... um... that's some washing I've been doing! Yes, that's it! It's just a panful of washing on the stove. It was very dirty and so I had to boil it to get it clean.'

The neighbour felt sure the old woman was not telling the truth, but she could hardly accuse her of telling lies, so she said, 'Oh dear. Never mind. I'll just come in for a chat anyway.'

Now the old woman knew she had been selfish in not offering to share her meal, but she knew she must not be rude to her neighbour, and turn her away, so she held open the door and her neighbour came in to the kitchen. They sat down comfortably, one on each side of the fireplace, and talked for a while. And then, perhaps because it was warm in the kitchen, or perhaps because she was tired, or even perhaps because she wanted to dream of delicious chicken soup, the old woman began to nod. Her eyes grew heavy and began to close, and in no time at all she was fast asleep.

Her neighbour wasted no time in tip-toeing to the stove and lifting the lid of the pan to see what was inside. Chicken soup. And dumplings! Just as she thought. It wasn't washing at all!

Silently, so as not to wake the old woman, she served herself a large bowlful of soup, and ate every last drop. Dumplings and all. Everything. Except the chicken bones. She left those in the pan.

Then she crept next door to her own house, and collected some dirty washing – some socks, a pillowcase and a nightdress. She tip-toed back with them. She filled the pan with water, stuffed the washing in it, put the pan back on the stove, and replaced the lid. Then she went home to her own house.

A long time later the old woman woke up.

'Good! She's gone home,' she said, looking round her kitchen. 'Now at last I can eat my soup. I'm really hungry now, I'm ready for a bowlful of delicious chicken soup.'

She went to the stove, lifted the lid of the pan... and stared at the contents in disbelief.

The conceited sea   *Pride/conceit*
adapted from Jewish mythology

At the beginning of time there was nothing. Then God decided to make the world. He created land and sea and sky. On the land he made mountains and valleys, soft earth and hard dry rock. To the sea he gave movement. He created huge waves and tiny ripples. He caused the sea to swell and turn, to rise and fall, to sweep in across the land, and to fall back deep in its bed.

As soon as the sea realised it could move, it swirled and swished and splashed and swooshed and swept up onto the land.

'Look at me,' it shouted. 'Look at how high I can go. Look at how strong and powerful I am. No-one can stop me. Look!' and it surged over the land, flooding the plains, filling the valleys, turning the soft earth to mud, and creeping higher and higher up the mountains.

'Stop!' shouted God. 'Enough! Go back to your sea-bed.' But the sea took no notice of God.

'I am the strongest thing there is,' it said. 'I am the most powerful thing in all creation. Nothing can stop me. I can flood all the world.'

When God heard the sea boasting like that, he became angry.

'If you don't stop showing off,' he said 'I shall send for the sands to fasten you in to your place.'

The sea laughed. 'The sands!' it said. 'And what can a few grains of sand do against me? Grains of sand are small, tiny, inconsequential things. I can push sand around with my smallest ripples. The sand could never fasten me down!' And as if to prove it, the sea swept further than ever across the land.

The grains of sand trembled and shivered when they heard the words of the sea. They knew they were tiny and helpless compared to the mighty ocean.

'You think the grains of sand are small and useless,' said God. 'And it's true that each one, by itself, is tiny, weak, insignificant. Each single grain of sand could never stand up against you. But if all the grains of sand joined together; if all the grains of sand became one; if all the grains of sand stood firm against you, they could be strong and powerful and even perhaps hold you in your place!'

'Never!' shouted the conceited sea. 'No-one is stronger than me.'

'We'll see,' said God. And he called to the four winds. 'Blow your hardest!' he commanded.

The four winds swept from their places in the sky. They gathered together in a twirling, swirling, tumbling frenzy. They whipped up and picked up every grain of sand they could find, and blew them in the direction of the sea.

The surface of the sea boiled and danced as the tiny grains of sand sliced into the waves. The sea went back a little. The sands piled up on the sea bed. The sea retreated a little more. The piles of sand grew, grain by grain, layer by layer, until they became beaches and dunes and hills and cliffs. The sea sank into its proper place and knew it must stay there.

'I'm sorry,' said the sea to God. 'I'm not the only powerful thing in your world. And now I know that small things can also be strong when they work together.'

Ever since that time, the sea has mostly stayed in its place, kept there by the grains of sand. Only occasionally does it forget the lesson that God taught it, and then it tries again to prove how strong it is.

cf. 'The sea and the sea-birds' on page 59. The stories are different, but in both the boastful sea is put in its place by a God.

The moon who wanted more *Conceit/pride/greed*
adapted from Jewish mythology

At the beginning of time, when God had just made the world and everything in it was new, the sun and the moon were equal. The sun was big and gold. The moon was large and silver. They were both as bright as each other and they were both extremely beautiful.

The sun and the moon took turns to shine. They each shone for the same length of time, and with the same power, and for a while all was well.

And then the moon began to want more.

'Why should I have to share the skies with *him*?' said the moon to herself. 'I want the sky to myself. Why should I have to hide for half the time? I want to shine *all* the time. I want to be brighter than the sun. I want to be bigger and more powerful. After all, I am much more beautiful than the sun, anyone can see that!'

The moon decided to go and tell God that she thought she should have more light, more time and more sky.

'And why is that?' asked God.

'Because I deserve more,' said the moon. 'I am better than the sun, and much more beautiful.'

'What do you want me to do?' asked God.

'I want you to make me bigger than the sun,' she said. 'I want you to make me brighter than him, and I want you to give me more time in the sky.'

'You are very conceited,' said God. 'You are very big-headed and full of your own importance. But I will certainly make some changes for you!'

As soon as God had spoken, the moon felt herself changing. She smiled to herself as she waited to grow larger and brighter. She wondered how it would feel, and she wondered what the sun would think when he saw what had happened. But the smile on her face soon turned to tears as she realised that she was not becoming bigger; on the contrary, she was shrinking and fading and fast disappearing.

'You are greedy,' said God angrily. 'So you will become smaller than the sun. You are conceited, so you will become less bright than the sun. You will pay for your greed and conceit for the rest of time.'

'I'm sorry,' cried the moon. 'I'm really sorry. I shouldn't have wanted more than my fair share. I shouldn't have been so big-headed. Please forgive me. Please put everything back to normal again.'

'No, I'm sorry, it's too late,' said God, gently. But he knew that the moon was truly sorry for the things she had said, and God didn't want to punish her further.

'You can have the stars to keep you company,' he said, and God sprinkled the dark sky with a thousand shining stars.

'And you can help mark the time,' said God. 'From this day forward, each day will start not with the sunrise, but with the appearance of the first three evening stars.'

And from that time on the Jewish people have counted the start of each day from the sight of the first three stars in the evening. They have counted their days and weeks, months and years, by the moon instead of the sun. And they have said special prayers to God, in the light of the moon, each time it is new in the sky.

The sea monster and the fox   *Greed/think for yourself*
adapted from Jewish mythology

There was once a sea monster who was so strong and wise, he was the king of all the waters and everything that lived in them. He was the ruler of the oceans and seas, the rivers and waterfalls, the fiords and estuaries, the lakes and ponds and pools and streams. He would have liked to have been the ruler of all the land animals, as well as all the sea creatures, but when God made the sea monster, he attached him to an invisible chain which prevented him from leaving the water. God knew how powerful the sea monster was, and knew that if he ever came on land, the sea would come with him and destroy everything it touched.

One day the sea monster heard that there was an animal on land, called a fox, which was wise and clever.

'I want him,' said the sea monster. 'I want to eat him so that I can have his wisdom.'

The sea monster ordered a large fish to swim to the shore, call for the fox, and bring him back for the sea monster to eat.

The fish set off. He waited near a place where he was told the fox would be. He waited for three days. On the fourth day the fish saw the fox, hunting, running along the sand dunes, chasing a rabbit. The rabbit escaped down a hole and the fox looked annoyed.

'Fox!' called the fish. 'Come over here! I have something important to tell you.'

The fox looked around and saw a sparkling silver fish in the sea, its head poking out of the waves.

'What do you want?' he asked.

'If you listen to me, you need never go hunting again,' said the fish. 'I saw how you just missed that rabbit, but if you come with me you can have as much to eat as you want, without having to catch it yourself.'

'What do you mean?' asked the fox.

'My king, the sea monster, is old and weak,' lied the fish. 'He's looking for someone to take over his kingdom, and he's heard how clever *you* are. He wants *you* to be king of the oceans after him.'

The fox listened carefully to this and thought it sounded wonderful – never to have to work again, never to have to hunt again, to live like a king and have servants to do everything.

'I'll come. I'll come,' he shouted. But then he added, 'But how? I can't swim.'

'No problem,' answered the fish. 'Just climb on my back and I'll take you to the sea monster. He's waiting for you.'

Without thinking the matter over, without considering what might happen, without giving the plan a second thought, the fox skipped across the sands and jumped aboard the fish's back.

'Off we go!' he shouted.

But soon the fox's joyful shouts turned to cries of terror and worry and anxiety. All around him was water. High waves. Foaming sea. Alien territory for a land animal. The taste of salt water was in his mouth and his fur was matted with salt sea spray.

'I don't like it,' he cried. 'Take me home.'

'No,' said the fish. 'And now I will tell you the truth. The sea monster isn't old or weak. He doesn't want you to be king after him. He wants to eat you so that he can have your wisdom.'

The fox thought quickly. He had to trick the fish into taking him back to shore, or he would certainly die.

'I wish I'd known the sea monster wanted to eat me,' he said to the fish. 'If I'd known I'd have brought my heart with me. It's where I keep my wisdom. I don't carry it round with me all the time, in case I lose it.'

The fish stopped swimming. 'You mean your heart isn't in your body?' he asked, amazed.

'Oh no,' said the fox. 'It's hidden in a cave near where you first saw me. Take me back there, and I'll get it for you.'

The fish turned round and swam back towards the shore. As soon as he reached the shallow waves at the water's edge, the fox jumped off the fish's back and splashed ashore.

'Hurry up!' said the fish. 'I don't want to keep the sea monster waiting.'

'You don't have to keep him waiting,' laughed the fox. 'You can go back to him straight away. But you can go without me. I'm not coming. You're not fooling me again! 'Bye!' and the fox scampered away inland, leaving the fish to go back and tell the sea monster that the fox was too clever to be caught.

The fox decided he'd had a narrow escape, and he made up his mind that in future, he would be content to do his own hunting and his own work, and not be taken in by promises of an easy life.

cf. 'The crocodile and the monkey', page 20. In this Buddhist version of the story, a monkey outwits a crocodile who is trying to steal his heart. 'The ape and the crocodile' is also found in Hindu folk-lore, although longer, and presented as a frame story to another, it is almost identical to the Buddhist version.

The man who lost himself   *Conceit/tolerance*
adapted from Jewish folk-lore

Once upon a time there was a man called Faivel, who was very absent-minded and forgetful. His memory was so bad that he could never even remember where he had put his clothes at bedtime, so every morning when he got dressed to go to synagogue, he was always late. Sometimes he would be ten minutes late, but sometimes it would be dinner time before he arrived.

Faivel went to synagogue every day, together with his friends and neighbours, to study the Torah. But here again Faivel's memory let him down. What he learned in the morning, he forgot by the evening. What he read one day, he'd forgotten the next. But, despite his poor memory, Faivel believed he was the best student of the Torah. He believed he understood its meaning better than any of the others, and he became very conceited.

'I know it all better than any of them,' he used to say to himself. 'It's a pity they are not able to grasp its meaning, to understand it all, as clearly as I do, but I must be patient with them, it's not their fault.'

Faivel became so conceited, so big-headed about his learning, that he was almost unbearable to be with. When the others gently tried to tell him that it was he, Faivel, who didn't understand, he wouldn't listen, but just smiled and said 'It's all right. I know you cannot help your lack of knowledge, just as I cannot help being so clever.'

One day, Faivel arrived later than ever at synagogue. He had been unable to find his hat or his coat, his shoes or his jacket, and had spent the entire morning searching for them.

'It's no good,' he said to himself as he hurried along to join the others. 'If I go on wasting time like this, I shall fall behind with my studies, and then I shall no longer be the cleverest man at the synagogue. Tonight when I go to bed I shall write down where I put everything. Then in the morning I'll be able to find all my clothes straight away, without having to spend hours searching for them.'

And that is exactly what Faivel did. At bedtime he got a piece of paper and a pencil and wrote 'The coat is on the back of the door' as he took off his coat and hung it up. Then he wrote 'The hat is on the table. The jacket is on the chair. The trousers are under the mattress. The shoes are by the fireplace.' Then for good measure he wrote 'The socks and underwear are in the top drawer,' although he usually remembered where they were, because he always put his clean clothes in the same place.

At last Faivel climbed in to bed, and as a joke he wrote 'I am in the bed', then he pushed the piece of paper under his pillow and went to sleep.

In the morning Faivel woke, and stretched, then found a crumpled piece of paper under his pillow.

'Oh yes,' he said. 'I remember.' He read the paper carefully, and the plan worked well. He easily found all his clothes. When he was fully dressed and ready to go out, Faivel checked the list again. The last line read 'I am in the bed'.

Faivel looked in the bed to see that he was there. But he wasn't! He wasn't in bed! Faivel looked all round the room, on the chair, in the wardrobe, under the table, but he was nowhere to be found.

'I'm missing,' he shouted. 'I've got lost in the night. I must go and look for myself.' And Faivel rushed out into the street to see if he could find himself.

He ran about searching behind walls, under bushes, over fences, inside buildings; making such a noise and commotion that all the neighbourhood came out to see what was going on.

'I'm lost,' wailed Faivel. 'I went to bed last night, and this morning when I looked, I'm not there anymore.'

'Of course you're not,' laughed the neighbours. 'You're not in bed because you're here, talking to us.'

'No, you don't understand,' cried Faivel. 'It's written on my list.' and he thrust his piece of paper into their hands.

'Look, it says 'I am in the bed' and I'm not. I know I'm not because I've looked, and I'm not there.'

'You are silly,' said one man. 'You're *here*. Now stop worrying, and go home.'

'No! I've lost myself. I can't go home until I'm found,' said Faivel.

'Don't be silly,' said the people. 'You're not lost. We can see you. We're talking to you. We know you're here.' But no matter how much the people tried to reassure Faivel, and tell him he was *not* lost, he refused to listen, refused to calm down, refused to understand.

At last one man in the crowd grew angry. 'You stupid man,' he shouted. 'I'll prove whether you're here or not. Take that! And that! And another!' and the man beat Faivel with a broom handle.

'Ow! That hurts,' yelled Faivel.

'You can feel it can you?' asked the man.

'Of course I can feel it,' said Faivel.

'Then if you can feel the pain, you must be there. You. In person. If you were lost, as you say you are, you wouldn't be able to feel the pain, would you?'

'You're right,' said Faivel. 'Thank you. Thank you so much. I don't know how you've done it, but you've found me again.'

'It wasn't too difficult,' said the man, smiling at his friends.

'I think perhaps I'm not the cleverest person in the world,' admitted Faivel. 'I think there are people around here who are more knowledgeable than me. It's just that I didn't realise it before.'

From that day on, Faivel was far less conceited and far more co-operative with his friends than he had ever been before. And strangely, the less conceited he became, the better his memory grew, until eventually he became quite skilled at understanding the Torah.

cf. 'The twelve men of Gotham' page 40. In this similar story, the twelfth man is thought to be missing because each man fails to count himself.

Further reading

For teachers

A Golden Treasury of Jewish Tales Asher Barash (W H Allen 1972)

Angels, Prophets, Rabbis and Kings from the Stories of the Jewish People Jose Paterson (Peter Lowe 1991)

Comparative Religions ed. W. Owen Cole (Blandford Press 1982)

Jewish Tales Leo Pavlat (Beehive Books 1986)

Six Religions in the Twentieth Century W. Owen Cole with Peggy Morgan (Hulton Educational 1984)

The Hasidic Story Book Harry M Rabinowicz (Shem Tov Publications London 1984)

The Power of Light – eight Stories for Hunukkah Isaac Bashevis Singer (Robson Books London 1983)

The Story of the Jewish People Vols 1 & 2 Gilbert & Libby Klaperman (Behrman House N.Y. 1957)

The Young Reader's Encyclopedia of Jewish History Viking Kestrel (1987)

When a Jew Celebrates Harry Gersh (Behrman House N.Y. 1971)

For children
I am a Jew Clive Lawton (Franklin Watts 1987)
Celebrations – Jewish Festivals Jane Cooper (Wayland 1989)
Our Culture – Jewish Jenny Wood (Franklin Watts 1988)
Stories from the Jewish World Sybil Sheridan (Macdonald 1987)
The Jewish World Douglas Charing (Macdonald 1983)
The Living Festivals Series – Passover, Chanukah (RMEP 1982)

Useful addresses

Central Jewish Lecture and Information Committee and Board of Deputies of British Jews. Fourth Floor, Woburn House, Upper Woburn Place, London WC1H OEP

Council of Christians and Jews. 1 Dennington Park Road, London NW6

Jewish Education Bureau. Director Douglas Charing. 8 Westcombe Avenue, Leeds LS8 2BS (Please send SAE with all requests.)

Study Centre for Christian-Jewish Relations. 17 Chepstow Villas, London W11 3DZ (Please send SAE with all requests.)

Primal Religions

There are believed to be between 200 and 300 million people living in Africa, the Americas and Australasia, who belong to 'traditional', 'pre-literate', 'ethnic' or 'tribal' societies. 'Primal' is a more accurate and acceptable description, since primal means fundamental or primary, and refers to those religions which existed prior to the world's universal religions. Historically, the primal religions lie behind all the universal religions and present a spiritual background that has been common to humankind throughout the ages.

Primal religions have no scriptures as such, and in primal societies religion and culture are almost one. Beliefs are handed down orally from one generation to the next. The specific beliefs vary from one society to another, and are dependant upon that society's immediate environment. Religion provides people with a framework within which they can find a meaning for life, and begin to understand and come to terms with their environment.

However, certain features are common to all the primal societies.

- The religions are all the serious attempts of adults to create a spiritual system which will support their society in life and in death.
- The religions are not 'missionary' in that the societies seek only to support themselves by way of their religions, and do not seek to convert others.
- The primal societies believe in a spiritual world of beings or powers which are stronger than humankind. The spirits are in all ordinary things and daily events.
- There is generally a humble view of humanity's place within the natural world.
- There is generally a belief in a Supreme Being or a High God, who has power to create all else. There is generally then a hierarchy of other powers or divinities, whose strengths interact with one another. It is humanity's place to attempt to live harmoniously with and amongst these powers.
- There is usually a belief in the living dead.

The primal societies are rich in story and myth. Humankind's most abstract thoughts in religion and art have been expressed in myth, and mythology itself has been described as 'philosophy in parables'. The subject of myths are often the great questions of life: How did we begin? Why are we here? What is the purpose of death? What lies beyond death itself?

The origin and purpose of myth are part of the story of human development itself, and many myths express people's primary explanations of the world in which they lived; of the forces which governed their lives, and the good or evil which befell or beset them. Many of these forces or powers were personified, and this personification was people's first step towards the formalisation of belief in religion.

Myths may appear 'childish', but because of their allegorical nature, they can contain profound truths and express serious beliefs. According to the psychologist Jung, myths are also of value because they contain clues to humankind's deepest hopes and fears, and reveal the depths of human nature.

Little was known in the West about primal societies until relatively recently. The first attempts to record these oral heritages were made by missionaries, traders, and (in the case of North America) government agents. Nineteenth century westerners tended to despise primal religions because they did not understand them and believed the religions at best to be a mere hotch-potch of superstitions and mumbo-jumbo. However, closer, more scientific and more objective study of the primal societies during the last 100 years, by anthropologists and ethnologists, has led to a greater understanding of the cultures and religions.

Nevertheless, even today, works on primal religions tend to be classified under anthropology, and not under religion, where they rightfully belong. There is also some disagreement as to *how* the material should be presented; anthropologists put forward the view that the stories must be accurately recorded and translated; narrators express the opinion that the literature – a living source – must be allowed to be adapted to meet the needs of today's audiences. The stories included here in *Share our World* are unashamedly my adaptations of traditional tales, and are among the most popular of the stories from the primal societies. However, I acknowledge that there is a place for accurate translations for scholarly study.

The tree with the difficult name
adapted from African fable

Small can be powerful

Once upon a time, a long time ago, there was a severe drought in Africa. The rains were waited for, and danced for, and prayed for, but still they didn't come. The animals were having great difficulty in finding enough food for them all.

One day, a gazelle came back from searching for food to say she had found a huge tree beyond the old water hole, out towards the mountain.

'But I've never seen a tree like it,' she said. 'It's enormous, and covered on every branch with big ripe juicy fruits. There's enough food on that tree to feed us all for weeks.'

'Let's go see it,' said the others, and so an enormous procession of animals paraded across the plain, beyond the old water hole, and out towards the mountain.

Sure enough, there was the tree, quite as big as the gazelle had said it was, and covered with fruits.

'But we can't eat the fruit,' said the lion. 'You all know the rule. We can only eat from a tree if we know the name of the tree. If we don't know its name, we may be poisoned by its fruit.'

The other animals agreed. Then one of them said, 'We must find out its name. That can't be too hard. The old woman who lives at the other side of the mountain will know. She knows everything.'

'We must choose the fastest animal to go and find her,' said the lion. 'The sooner we know the name of the tree, the sooner we can begin to eat its fruit and put an end to our hunger. Send the hare. He's a fast runner.'

And so the hare was sent to find the old woman who lived at the other side of the mountain, and to ask her the name of the tree. He found her straight away, without any difficulty, and she told him that the tree was called an Oowungelema Tree, and that, yes, it would be quite safe to eat the fruit.

The hare ran back to the animals as quickly as he could, saying to himself over and over again, 'Oowungelema, Oowungelema'. But, just as he was in sight of the animals, the hare tripped and fell over a dead branch, and the name of the Oowungelema Tree went clean out of his head.

'You silly animal,' said the lion. 'We'll send the gazelle this time, she can run just as fast as you.'

So the gazelle was sent to find the old woman who lived at the other side of the mountain.

'The tree is the Oowungelema Tree,' said the old woman. 'Keep remembering the name all the way home. Don't forget it!'

The gazelle said she wouldn't, and she set off to tell the animals the tree's name. But on the way, she saw a tiny new born fawn, and stopped to say hello. By the time she arrived back home she had completely forgotten the name of the tree.

'You silly animal,' said the lion. 'I can see there is no alternative but for me to go myself. I can be there and back in no time, for I'm a fast runner, and I won't forget!'

The lion found the old woman with no difficulty and was told the name of the tree. He set off at a smart pace back to the animals, reciting to himself over and over again 'Oowungelema-Tree, Oowungelema-Tree, Oowungelema-three, Two-one-get-me-my-tea, One-two-hot-in-my-tree, Three-two-one-in-a-tree,' until he had made utter nonsense of what he had been told, and had mixed up the name so much that he couldn't remember how it had been to begin with.

The animals were not pleased.

'You are supposed to be our king,' they said. 'You are not supposed to get things wrong,' they said. 'I'm sorry,' said the lion. 'Let's send another animal instead.'

So they sent the bison, then the buffalo; they sent the hyena and the giraffe; they sent the elephant and the monkey and the rat and the tiger and the antelope and the rhinoceros and the mongoose and the zebra and even the mouse. In fact they sent every animal that could run, but not one single animal could manage to remember the name of the Oowungelema Tree, and bring the name home to the other animals.

'I could go,' said the tortoise.

'You?' said the other animals.

'Yes. Me.' said the tortoise.

'You can't run,' said the lion.

'Well, *you* can't remember!' said the tortoise.

The lion felt very put out at this, but he knew that it was true, so he agreed to let the tortoise try.

'It's a waste of time,' said the other animals. 'He's so stupid and slow and silly and small, *he* won't be able to do it. If *we* couldn't, then *he* certainly won't be able to!'

The tortoise set off on his slow small legs, and eventually arrived at the home of the old woman at the other side of the mountain.

'Tell me the name of the tree please,' he said. 'The others all tried but none of them remembered.'

'I expect they were all too fast,' said the wise old woman. 'You see, sometimes going slowly gets you there quicker in the end! You go slowly, and as you go, remember the name of the Oowungelema Tree. Take care now.'

The tortoise set off again. He plodded. Step after step. It was a long way. He was very tired. He nearly gave up. But he kept on going. At last he saw the animals waiting for him under the Oowungelema Tree. He struggled the last few steps and the animals came to help him.

'Well?' they asked.

'Oowungelema Tree,' whispered the tortoise.

At the sound of its name, the tree showered the animals with rich juicy delicious fat fruits to eat. And the animals gave the first fruit to the tortoise.

'Thank you,' they said to him.

cf. Aesop's 'The hare and the tortoise', in which the two animals run a race. The hare races off but later falls asleep, the tortoise – slow and steady – wins the race.

See also 'The tortoise and the hare' (page 108) which is an African version of the story.

The tortoise and the hare

adapted from African fable

Strongest may not be the most clever/conceit

One day the hare was boasting, as usual, about how far he could jump, and how high, and how fast, and how fast he could run and how far, and how well, when the tortoise decided he had heard enough.

'I'm tired of listening to you,' he said. 'Your conversation is always the same – what you can do, how fast you can run, how far you can jump. Well I've heard enough. I'm going to put a stop to your boasting!'

'Oh yes?' said the hare. 'And how exactly are you going to do that?'

'I'm going to challenge you to a competition,' said the tortoise.

The hare burst out laughing. 'You! Challenge me! To a competition! And I suppose you want me to give you a head start of at least a couple of months,' and he began to laugh all over again at his own joke.

'No,' said the tortoise. 'I want to challenge you to a jumping competition. We'll meet here tomorrow and we'll both jump. Everyone can watch, and we'll see who can jump the farthest.'

'Right!' said the hare. ''Till tomorrow.'

That night, the tortoise asked his wife to go as quickly as she could to a place in the bushes that he pointed to, and then to wait until he gave the shout in the morning. His wife set off, and by dawn the next day she had arrived at the place, and she hid in the bushes.

In the morning the tortoise went to meet the hare as arranged.

'Ready?' asked the hare, who was already there.

'Ready!' said the tortoise. 'You go first hare. Jump over there,' and he pointed towards some bushes in the distance.

The hare leapt with a great boisterous bound high into the air, and landed a good way away.

'My turn now,' shouted the tortoise at the top of his voice. 'Here I go!' and he slid silently into the thick grass next to where he stood.

'I'm here,' shouted his wife from the bushes, a good way beyond where the hare had landed.

The hare stared at the tortoise – or rather at the tortoise's wife.

'How did you do that?' he said. 'You never jumped as far as that! Anyway, I didn't see you jump. You must have cheated!'

'Cheated?' said the tortoise. 'Me? Of course not! I just jumped so quickly that you never saw me, that's all!'

The hare was somehow not convinced, but gave the tortoise the benefit of the doubt. However, he challenged the tortoise to a running race. He knew he would win that.

'Yes,' said the tortoise. 'I'll run a race with you, but not today. I can't run a race today. I'm far too tired with all that jumping. I'll race with you tomorrow. Same time, same place.'

The hare agreed to run the race the next day, and went home to have a sleep so that he would be ready for it. (He'd heard once, of a hare who'd lost a race by falling asleep in the middle of it!)

The tortoise also went home, but not to sleep. He gathered together all the members of his family, and spent the entire night putting them in certain positions along the path, and telling them what to do in the morning.

The next day the hare was at the starting post bright and early. The tortoise came plodding along at the appointed time. They lined up at the start. Ready. Steady. GO!

The hare streaked away as fast as lightning and was immediately way ahead of the tortoise.

'Tortoise!' he called back, over his shoulder.

'Yes, I'm here,' called a voice ahead of him.

For a moment the hare froze in his tracks. Surely not. The tortoise couldn't possibly be ahead of him. He leaped away again, as fast as he had ever run in his life. Once again he called back over his shoulder, 'Tortoise?'

'Yes, I'm here, I'm winning,' called the tortoise's voice from ahead of him.

This could not be true.

The hare sped on further.

'Tortoise?' he called back.

'I'm here,' called the voice from ahead.

And so it went on all the way round the path.

At last the hare arrived back at the starting post, puffing and panting and almost at the point of exhaustion, to find the original tortoise calmly waiting for him.

'Hello,' said the tortoise. 'What took you so long?'

The hare collapsed in a heap on the ground and promised himself he would never boast again for as long as he lived... or at least until he got his breath back!

cf. Aesop's 'The stag and the hedgehog' in which the two animals argue and are asked to run a race to settle the dispute. Since the stag has already cheated, the female hedgehog decides that her mate will be at the start of the race, and she will be at its finish. Neither the stag nor the boar (arbiter) discover how the hedgehog managed to run so quickly!

See also notes at the end of 'The tree with the difficult name' (page 107).

The turkey girl
adapted from North American legend

Many years ago, in a place near Thunder Mountain, lived a girl. She was very poor and had almost nothing in the world – no family, no home, no friends, no possessions. But she did have a job. It didn't pay much, but it was a job nevertheless. The girl was a Turkey Girl; she looked after a flock of turkeys for the rich people who owned them.

The girl ate with the turkeys and lived with them. You see, they were the only friends she had. She was kind to them, and took good care of them. She never beat them, or chased them, or hurt them. She cared for them as though they were her own family.

'You are the only family I have,' she would say to them.

The Turkey Girl often talked to the birds. She would tell them all her secrets, all her wishes, all her dreams. She never minded telling the turkeys her secret thoughts, because after all, they were birds not people, so they couldn't understand what she was saying.

One day the Turkey Girl overheard some news: there was to be a festival of dance in the town in a few days' time – a grand festival to which all the important people in the neighbourhood would be invited.

'I wish I could go,' she told the turkeys. 'It'll be wonderful. There'll be music and singing and dancing and delicious food. But I can't go looking like this,' and she looked at her ragged clothes and her dirty skin.

During the next days the Turkey Girl watched the townspeople prepare for the festival. The ladies had beautiful new gowns made, and the men ordered their tailors to make smart new suits. The cooks made cakes and savouries for the festival, and everyone in the town talked and laughed about the exciting event to come.

The Turkey Girl told the turkeys all about everything that was happening, and they listened with solemn faces.

Suddenly, to the girl's astonishment, the largest turkey spoke.

'You have been kind to us, and now we want to repay you. We will arrange for you to go to the festival dance, but you must listen carefully to what we say.'

The girl promised that she would, and the turkeys told her to take off her coat.

She did as she was asked, and took off her old, torn, threadbare coat and handed it to the turkeys. They spread it out on the ground and one of the turkeys stepped forward and pecked and pecked at it. The most beautiful gold and silver embroidery, dotted with sequins and pearls, appeared on the coat, which by now had turned into white silk. In minutes the coat was ready and the Turkey Girl put it on. It was a coat fit for a princess.

'Now give me your dress,' said the turkey.

Again the girl did as she was asked, and again the turkeys spread out the garment on the ground. Another turkey stepped forward and began to peck. The faded cotton dress turned into exquisite silver silk, and the most beautiful gold and white embroidery, sprinkled with diamonds, appeared on it.

'Now your shoes,' said the turkey, and the shabby shoes were changed into white satin slippers with silver stitching. Then the turkeys brushed the Turkey Girl with their wings until her skin was as clean and smooth as the inside of an egg shell, and her hair as soft as a swan's wing.

'Now', said the turkey, 'Off you go to the dance, but don't stay too late. And, before you go, open the gate for us, because who knows, you may forget us when you are with the grand people at the dance.'

'I won't forget you,' promised the Turkey Girl. 'And I won't stay too late.'

The Turkey Girl opened the gate and set off for the dance. And all the people she met marvelled at how beautiful she was.

'Who can she be?' they asked.

'She's not from round here,' they said.

'We've never seen her before,' they declared.

The Turkey Girl had a wonderful time at the dance. All the young men wanted to dance with her and she danced with every one of them in turn. She ate foods she had never seen before, and tasted drinks she'd never heard of. She had such a wonderful time at the dance that she never gave a thought to the time, or to the turkeys, or to the promise she had made.

It wasn't until the night turned to morning and the first misty grey fingers of dawn came creeping across the sky, that the Turkey Girl remembered her promise.

'I won't forget you, and I won't stay too late,' she had said. The Turkey Girl ran from the dancing young men; ran and ran as fast as she could, along the lanes and through the gate, back to her turkeys.

'I'm here,' she called. 'I'm sorry I'm late. I didn't really forget you.'

But there was no answer from the turkeys. They had gone; away through the open gate, across the plains, and over the mountain, because they knew that the girl had forgotten them, that she had stayed too late at the dance.

The Turkey Girl stood in her rags once more, and cried. She cried for what might have been, she cried for her turkeys, and she cried for herself.

cf. Grimm's tale of Cinderella. There are clear similarities between the well-known fairy tale and this Indian Cinderella story. However, there is no 'happy ever after' in this version. The ending is much more severe than its European counterpart.

The tar man

Pride/laziness/forgiveness

adapted from Black American Legend

Once upon a time there was a terrible drought, and all the streams and rivers, lakes and water holes dried up. The animals were in danger of dying of thirst, so they called a meeting to decide what should be done.

Every animal was there from the largest to the smallest, because of course, the lack of water affected them all. Eventually, after a great deal of discussion, it was decided that they should all help to dig a well.

'With a well, dug deep into the earth, we shall have plenty of water,' they said. 'The work will be hard, but if we all join in and help, we'll be able to do it.'

Every animal agreed to do his or her best to help with digging the well. Everyone that is, except the rabbit. He was lazy and never liked to work at the best of times, and especially not when it was *hard* work.

'You can get on with the job without me,' he said to the others. 'I'll just have a drink of water from the well when you've finished it!'

'If you don't help us to dig the well, you're not having any water from it,' said the other animals.

'Oh no? We'll see about that!' laughed the rabbit, and he lay down to sleep in the shade whilst the other animals got on with the work.

Eventually the well was dug and the animals all had a deep drink of the cool clear water. The rabbit watched them.

'You needn't think you're having any of our water,' said the monkey. 'I'm going to guard this well tonight. You can go and find your own water if you're thirsty.' The rabbit said nothing, but carried on watching as the other animals all set off for home, leaving the monkey guarding the well.

For a long time nothing happened. Then the rabbit began to sing. Very softly and gently. Very tunefully. Very quietly. The monkey listened to the music. He didn't recognise the rabbit's voice. He'd never heard the rabbit sing before. He didn't know the rabbit could sing the most magically beautiful songs. The monkey stood up and began to dance, slowly first, then faster, faster, away from the well and out over the fields. The rabbit skipped to the well, and drank a long, slow, cool, clear drink.

In the morning the other animals came to the well to find the monkey gone, the rabbit asleep under the tree where they'd last seen him, and rabbit footprints all round the edge of the well.

'He's drunk our water!' cried the bear. 'And where's that good-for-nothing monkey? I'll make sure that rabbit doesn't steal our water tonight. *I'll* guard the well.'

'But you might disappear like the monkey,' said the giraffe. 'We need another plan.'

'We need to make a tar man,' said the lion. 'That'll teach the rabbit not to steal our water.'

The animals waited until later in the day when the rabbit was out of sight. Then, without him seeing, they bundled some sticks together in the shape of a man, and covered it with sticky, black, gluey, gooey tar. They set the tar man to guard the well, and all went away to their own homes.

A little while later, the rabbit came back to his place under the tree. He saw the man guarding the well.

For a long time the rabbit did nothing. Then he began to sing a soft and gentle song. He waited for the man to take notice of the song, but the man stood straight and still as though he couldn't hear the beautiful singing.

The rabbit came a little closer to the man and sang his song again. The man stood straight and still and took no notice.

The rabbit came and stood in front of the man and sang his song again.

Nothing. No reaction at all.

'Well!' grumbled the rabbit. 'You're the first one to take no notice of my magical voice. Don't you like my song?'

The man said nothing. He just stared straight ahead.

'Listen to me!' shouted the rabbit. 'Everyone listens to me when they hear my singing.'

But the man just stared ahead.

'You'll be sorry if you don't listen to me,' yelled the rabbit. 'I'll punch you and I'll kick you and I'll fight you until you lie down dead on the ground.' And in temper the rabbit flew at the man and punched him and kicked him for all he was worth.

But no sooner did the rabbit touch the tar man, than he stuck fast to the sticky, black, gluey, gooey tar. His paws, his front legs, his back legs, his fur, and even his head and ears, were held quite tight to the tar man. The more the rabbit struggled and fought to get free, the more the sticky black tar held him fast.

'Help! Help!' he shouted. 'I've been captured. I've been kidnapped. I'm stuck.'

The animals came and looked at him stuck fast to the tar man. They lifted him down and set him stiffly on the ground again. They told him it served him right for being too clever, too big-headed, too lazy. They sent him to go and clean his fur, and gave him some of their water to wash with.

The rabbit said thank you, and promised in future to help them any time they wanted to dig a well!

This is one of many different versions of the 'tar baby' story, believed to originate in Africa. A Nigerian version of the story tells of a spider who sticks to a girl made of resin from the rubber tree. In a different Nigerian tale, a hare is caught by the rubber girl, whilst in a version of the story from Angola, a hare and a monkey are tricked by a leopard into sticking to a wooden girl smeared with gum. In a

southern *African story a hare adheres to a sticky-backed tortoise which is hiding at
the bottom of a well.*

*The rabbit in African fable is the humorous trickster portrayed by the jackal of
Indian fable or the fox of Aesop.*

The lord of the winds
adapted from an Innuit legend

Honesty/doing your best

Far away in the north, in the land of the Eskimos, lived a man and his two
daughters. They lived in a tent made of animal skins, which barely kept out the
icy wind and snows at the best of times, but when the great blizzard began, they
feared they would freeze to death. The wind whipped through the camp, and
no-one dared to set foot outside their tent. All they could do was to huddle
together inside and wait for the blizzard to die away.

But the blizzard continued, all day, all night, the next day, the following night,
on and on as though it was never going to stop.

The people began to despair of ever going outside again, of ever seeing the
sun again, of even staying alive.

'We must do something to make the storm stop,' said the man, 'Or we shall
die.'

'But *we* can do nothing,' said the girls.

'We must go and see the Lord of the Winds,' said their father. 'The storm is
raging like this because he is angry for some reason. One of you must visit the
Lord of the Winds, and find out why he is angry. Perhaps then the storm will
stop.'

The man sent his eldest daughter out into the storm, to go and find the Lord of
the Winds.

'Follow the north wind,' he said. 'Don't stop for anything. At the other side of
the mountain, look for a small bird. When you see it, offer to shelter it in your
hand, and it will tell you which way to go.'

The girl stepped out into the north wind and began to trudge through the
snow. She was so cold she could no longer feel her feet or fingers. The wind tore
at her coat and blew splinters of ice in her face. The girl stopped at the top of the
mountain to tie her coat more tightly round herself, then began to walk down the
far side. A small brown bedraggled bird flew around her head, but she flapped it
away with her hands and it disappeared into the dark sky.

Much much later, the girl found an empty tent, all by itself in the snow. The
Lord of the Winds came swirling out of it and shouted 'What do you want?'

'Make the storm stop,' she said. 'It's too cold, too fierce, for the people of my
camp.'

'If I am to do something for you, then you must do something for me,' said the
Lord of the Winds. 'Take this food to the old woman who lives across the valley,'

and he handed the girl a dish of meat.

Once more the girl stepped out into the storm. But she had only walked a few steps, when she stopped.

'I am not walking all that way,' she said. 'He won't know whether I've been to the old woman's or not!' And she threw the meat into the snow, and went back to the Lord of the Winds.

He looked in the empty dish and asked her what the old woman had given her in return for the food. The girl turned pale, for she realised that he knew she had not done as she had been asked.

The Lord of the Wind then gave the girl some animal skins, and told her to make him a new coat out of them.

'I can't do that,' cried the girl. 'I don't know how to.'

'Then outside with you!' he shouted, and he pushed her out of the tent. The girl fell into a snowdrift and there she froze to death.

The girl's father and her younger sister waited and waited for the blizzard to stop, but when it showed no sign of doing so, the man said to his younger daughter 'I fear she has not done what I asked. She has not done her best, and the storm still rages; the Lord of the Winds must still be angry. You, my youngest child, must go and find him. You must ask him to make the storm cease. But remember all that I have said, and follow my instructions carefully. Then perhaps our people will be saved.'

The youngest girl set out into the dreadful storm. The wind tore at her coat and snow filled her boots, but she remembered the words of her father and she kept on walking. As she crossed the mountain top, a tiny brown bedraggled bird fluttered around her head, and she held out her hands to it and sheltered it from the storm. It led her to the home of an old woman.

The woman gave the girl a needle made of bone and a sharp knife, and told her to take them to the tent of the Lord of the Winds. The bird showed her the way, and soon she came to a tent, standing alone in the vast expanse of ice and snow.

The Lord of the Winds roared out of the tent and shouted, 'Why are you here? What do you want?'

'Please make the storm stop,' said the girl. 'The people where I live are afraid that they will die, because the winds are so strong and cold, and the storm is so fierce. Please make it stop.'

'If I do that for you,' said the Lord of the Winds, 'Then you must do something for me. Here are some fur skins. Make me a coat to keep me warm.'

The girl used the knife and the needle the old woman had given her, and began to make the Lord of the Winds a new coat. The work was difficult and soon her fingers were sore and aching, but she persevered. She kept on working. She didn't give up. At last the coat was finished and the Wind Lord was pleased with it. 'You have worked well,' he said. 'Thank you.'

As the Lord of the Winds said those words, the storm died down and the sun began to shine. Back in the camp, the girl's father and their neighbours came out of their tents and gave thanks that his youngest daughter had saved them from the blizzard.

Foolish John   *Tolerance/small can be powerful*
adapted from a North American folk-tale

There was once a young man who did everything so oddly – so differently from everyone else – that all the people called him Foolish John, and forgot what his real name was. Foolish John used to do most things backwards, or at the wrong time, or in a different order from everyone else; and I'm afraid everyone used to laugh at him.

For example, Foolish John always took out his umbrella when the sun shone, but when it rained he used to take off his hat and coat and sit outside in a deck-chair. And everyone used to laugh.

In winter, Foolish John wore hardly any clothes, but in summertime when it was hot, he would wear a pullover and a jumper, three pairs of trousers, four pairs of socks, two scarves, a woolly hat and an overcoat. And everyone used to laugh.

Foolish John always went to bed when the sun rose, and got up just as it began to get dark. He walked backwards wherever he went, and he carried a mirror so that he could see where he was going. And everyone used to laugh.

One day the king heard about Foolish John,

'Send him to the palace,' ordered the king. 'He can come and amuse me and my court. I like something I can laugh at!'

So Foolish John was taken to the palace and put in front of the king. The king and the courtiers teased him and poked fun at him. They bullied him and called him unkind names. Then they laughed even louder.

'Oh, this is *fun*,' shouted the king. 'It is so easy to laugh at you because you are so stupid.' And he laughed until tears rolled down his face. But some people in the king's palace began to feel uncomfortable. They thought the king was being too cruel, too unkind to Foolish John. But they dared not say anything in case they angered the king.

The king knew nothing of how some of his people felt, and he carried on teasing Foolish John.

'Have you always been stupid? Do you always look so silly? Why are you so tall and thin? You look like a beanpole, or a piece of spaghetti, or a length of string. Come on boy, speak! Have you lost your voice, or left your tongue behind? You *can* talk I suppose?'

Foolish John felt too miserable to speak. He hung his head and said nothing.

The king went on 'Well! If you won't *answer* my questions, perhaps you'd like to *ask* me one. That'd be good! You asking me a question.' And the king began to laugh all over again at the thought of Foolish John asking him a sensible question.

'I know', boasted the king, so that everyone could hear, 'ask me a question that I can't answer, and I'll give you half my kingdom,' and he burst out laughing again, because Foolish John couldn't possibly ask the king a question he couldn't answer... Or could he?

Slowly, Foolish John lifted up his head and looked the king in the eye.

'Not one question, but three,' he said. 'Three questions you will not be able to answer.'

The king turned purple with rage at the impertinence of the boy. The rest of the courtiers grew silent.

'What gets wetter as it dries?' Foolish John asked.

'And what has no top and no bottom, no left and no right?' he said.

'And what is at the end of your kingdom?'

The king said nothing for a long time. Then he grew red and began to shout. 'Those are not proper questions. You're cheating. How am I expected to know the answers to such stupid questions. Yes, that's it. You are stupid and your questions are stupid. I take back my challenge.'

'But sir,' said one of the courtiers. 'The boy has done what you asked. A riddle question is a question nevertheless. Can you answer the questions, or not?

'No!' shouted the king, 'Because there *is* no answer.'

'There is,' said Foolish John quietly. 'A towel gets wetter as it dries, a ball has no top, no bottom, no left and no right, and at the end of your kingdom... is the letter M!'

'He's right,' shouted the people. 'He's right. He's beaten the king. He's not as silly as he seems. In fact he's very clever. Give him half the kingdom as promised.'

And so it was that Foolish John was given half the king's kingdom, and his real name back – as people suddenly remembered what it was. The people also suddenly remembered that it's cruel to laugh at others, and that silly people are often not as silly as they seem.

The argument
adapted from an African folk tale   *Honesty/fair play/greed*

Once upon a time, a rich man lived in a village in Africa with his wife and young son. One day the man became very ill, and he knew he would soon die. He wanted to make sure that his wife and son were cared for after his death, so he called his neighbour, Osai, to his side and asked him to help.

'Osai, I want you to look after my family. Make sure they are well cared for until my son is old enough to go out to work. Will you do this for me? I am leaving you plenty if money to look after them. Will you make sure they are all right?'

'Of course I will,' said Osai. But something in Osai's voice made the rich man suspicious. He believed Osai might cheat his wife and son out of their lands and money, so he called his wife to see him.

'I will soon die,' he said to her. 'But you and our boy, Marimba, will be cared for. I have asked Osai, our neighbour, to look after you both until Marimba is old enough to work. Here is a locket. I want you to put it round Marimba's neck. He must never take it off, for inside is a list of all my lands and animals. If anyone tries to cheat you out of what is yours, this piece of paper will prove what is right.'

After the rich man died, Osai told Marimba and his mother to go and live in a tumbledown hut. He gave them a tiny amount of money each week, which was barely enough for them to live on, whilst he, Osai, lived like a king in the rich man's house. He took all the rich man's land and animals for his own. The rich man's wife complained to Osai, but he told her she should be grateful she was being cared for at all, and to be quiet or he would throw her out with nothing.

Many years later, when Marimba became a man, he took the piece of paper from inside the locket his father had given him, and went to see Osai.

'You have cheated us for long enough,' he said. 'Now it is time for you to give us back the lands and the animals that are rightfully ours. I have a list here, which my father wrote out, and which proves to the world that all the things you have taken belong to my mother and me. Give us back those things that are ours!'

'What rubbish you talk,' shouted Osai. I have nothing that is yours. Everything I have is my own. Give me that piece of paper.' And Osai snatched the piece of paper from Marimba, stuffed it into his mouth, and ate it.

'There!' he said. 'You have no proof now. Be off with you, and never speak to me again.'

When Marimba went home and told his mother what had happened, she said 'Then you must go and see the chief of the village. He will have to sort it out. Osai cannot get away with this deceit and dishonesty any longer.'

So Marimba went to see the chief of the village, and explained to him exactly what had happened since the death of his father many years earlier.

The chief of the village then called for Osai to come and see him; but Osai did not tell the truth. He told the chief that Marimba and his mother were lying, that he had only the lands and animals that were his, and that he wouldn't dream of taking anything that didn't belong to him.

The chief of the village didn't know who to believe. At last he said 'Come here, to this place, in the morning. Osai, bring your wife. Marimba, bring your mother. I know how we can sort this out!'

The next morning, the chief of the village was standing outside his house, next to a large wooden box, when Osai and his wife, and Marimba and his mother arrived.

'What's that for?' asked Osai.

'You are to carry this box right round the village,' said the chief. 'Marimba, you and your mother will go first. Osai, you and your wife will stay here until they are back. Go.'

Marimba and his mother picked up the heavy wooden box between them. They struggled down the road with it. The sun burned down on them and they became hotter and hotter.

'I can't carry this much further,' said Marimba's mother.

'Yes you must,' said Marimba. 'If carrying this box is going to prove Osai has cheated us, then the effort will be worth it.'

'You are right,' said his mother, and they carried the box right round the village, to arrive back where they started, hot and exhausted.

'Now your turn,' said the chief of the village, turning to Osai and his wife.

They hoisted the box up and set off down the road. The sun burned down.

'I can't carry this thing,' grumbled Osai's wife.

'You must,' said Osai. 'The chief must never know that I cheated on Marimba's lands and animals. He must never know that I swallowed that list. Now get a move on,' and Osai kicked his wife to make her walk faster. Soon they arrived back where they started.

'So what did that prove?' asked Osai.

'I'll show you what that proved,' said the chief, and he opened the heavy wooden box. Out climbed the village medicine man, who told the chief exactly what the four people had said as they walked round the village with the box.

'That's it then,' said the chief. 'Osai, you are a thief and a liar. You will give Marimba back all that is his. You will pay him extra for all the upset you have caused him and his mother, and *you* will go and live in the tumbledown hut with nothing. Go!'

And so it was that Marimba and his mother were given back all the lands, animals and money that were theirs by right, and Osai, who had cheated, got nothing.

Mgumba and the djin   *Laziness*
adapted from a Nigerian legend

Mgumba was a lazy man who would much rather sit in the sun and day-dream than work for his living. His wife had to nag him all the time to get him to do any work at all.

One day Mgumba was out looking for firewood, when he came upon a fine field he had never seen before.

'That would be a good field for me,' he said. 'With a field like that I could be a rich man. I wish it was mine.'

'It can be if you like!' said a voice at Mgumba's side. 'You can have this field if you want it. It's yours.'

Mgumba looked round but could see nothing.

'No, you can't see me,' said the voice. 'I'm invisible, but I'm here. Come back tomorrow and we'll talk again.'

Mgumba hurried home to tell his wife the good news about the invisible voice and the field that was now his.

'You stupid man,' shouted his wife when she heard. 'Don't you know that your "invisible voice" was a djin – a wicked spirit who can do you harm? Don't you go anywhere near that field again, do you hear me?'

'I hear you,' said Mgumba. But the next morning he took no notice of his wife's advice, and hurried to the fine field.

'I think I'll plant corn in this field,' said Mgumba to himself. 'It looks like a good field for corn.'

'It is,' said a voice by Mgumba's side. 'Why don't you start to dig it?'

So Mgumba began to dig the field, but no sooner had he started than the strangest thing happened. The djin snatched the spade out of his hand, and began to do the digging. But of course, since the djin was invisible, it looked as though the spade was digging all by itself. Mgumba sat back and watched.

'This is good,' he said. 'All my work is being done, and I haven't had to lift a finger – or even a spade,' and he chuckled to himself.

During the next weeks, Mgumba discovered that whatever job he started, the djin took over and finished. Mgumba didn't have to do any hard work. Mgumba planted one seed; the djin planted a fieldful. Mgumba pulled out one weed; the djin pulled out a hundred. Mgumba threw away one stone from the soil; the djin cleared them all.

Soon the field was waving with ripening golden corn and Mgumba decided he must bring his wife to see it. 'She will see that she was wrong to tell me never to come back here,' he said. 'She will see that the djin is good, and not a wicked spirit like she said.'

Mgumba went home for his wife and brought her back to see the field of corn.

'Look!' he said. 'See how good it is, and see how hard the djin works. He does whatever I do. Watch!' And Mgumba picked up the watering can to water one plant. Instantly the watering can flew from his hands and zipped up and down the rows of plants, sprinkling clear fresh drops of water as it went.

While the djin was watering the field, Mgumba – without thinking – broke off an ear of corn, and dropped it on the soil. Suddenly the watering can fell to the ground and the djin began to break off the ears of corn. Soon every stem of beautiful ripening corn was snapped off and thrown to the ground.

'NO!' shouted Mgumba. 'You're not to do that. Oh look at my lovely corn, my beautiful field. You've ruined it. STOP!' But it was too late. The djin had completed what Mgumba had begun, just as he had with the other jobs.

Mgumba was distraught. And in his distress he blamed his wife.

'It's all your fault,' he shouted. 'The djin was helping me before you came.'

'It's not my fault,' said Mgumba's wife. 'And you know it. That djin is wicked.

You should know by now that there is no easy short-cut to hard work. The djin has tricked you.'

'He's not tricked me,' shouted Mgumba. And then he did something he had never done before; he hit his wife because he was so angry.

Immediately, the djin began to hit her too. She couldn't see where the blows were coming from, but she could feel them. Mgumba's wife fell to the ground and tried to shield herself from the dreadful blows. Mgumba again shouted to the djin to stop, but just as before, it took no notice.

Mgumba quickly put his arms round his wife and helped her to her feet. He half pulled her, half carried her, out of the field and away from the djin. At last they were out of reach of the dreadful blows.

'I'm sorry,' said Mgumba. 'I should have listened to you. I should have known that you can't grow corn by magic, you can only do it through hard work. I promise you I'll never be lazy again.'

And as far as anyone can tell, Mgumba kept his promise, and was never lazy again.

This theme, where a spirit of some kind helps those who are good, but brings trouble to those who are lazy, unkind or ungrateful, is found throughout the world.

cf. Grimm's 'The elves and the shoemaker', the Russian fairy tale of 'Vassilissa', and more recently, Beatrix Potter's 'The Tailor of Gloucester'.

The packages   *Obedience/honesty*
adapted from a North American Indian legend

Once upon a time a warrior came back from the wars. He was weary of war, and tired of travelling. All he wanted now was a quiet life, a home to settle down in.

'I'd like to be a farmer,' he said. 'A farmer leads a good life. He has plenty of fresh air and exercise, yet he stays in the same place. He puts down roots. I'll be a farmer.'

The warrior found a piece of land and made a home, and then began to think about what to grow on his land.

'But I cannot grow anything,' he said. 'To grow something I need seeds, and I have none. Seeds come from the ripe plants, and I have no plants, so I have no seeds. Whatever shall I do?'

Just then Messou, the great rabbit came bounding up to the warrior-farmer.

'I can help,' he said. 'I can bring you many seeds, then you can plant which you want.'

'Can you bring me them soon?' asked the farmer.

'I will bring them tomorrow,' said Messou.

The next day, Messou came to the farmer's home, carrying a basket full of small packages. He tipped them all out on to the ground. There were a great many of them, all tied like parcels with thin string. Messou started to count them out and to explain what each package contained.

'But this one', he said, pointing to a tiny package, 'is not filled with seeds. This one has a pinch of immortality in it – a little everlasting life. On no account are you ever to open it. If you do, all kinds of dreadful things will happen. You must put the package in a safe place, and simply forget that it is there. Neither you, nor anyone else must open it. Do you understand?'

'Yes,' said the farmer. 'But if I am not to open it, why are you giving it to me?'

'To save,' said Messou. 'But you must remember never to look inside. Can you promise that? Can you promise never to open it?'

'Of course I promise,' said the farmer. 'I can keep a promise. I can keep my word.'

'Make sure you do,' said Messou, and picking up his empty basket, he left the farmer to his planting.

Soon there were fields of crops growing on the farm. All the seeds that Messou had brought had been planted, and the special package that must never be opened, had been put in a safe place. But the farmer could not forget about it. Every day he thought about the strange parcel. Every night he went to sleep wondering what was inside.

One day, the farmer brought the tiny packet out of its safe place and spent a long time looking at it. Then he turned it over and over in his hands. He felt the paper of the package and the thin string that was tying it together. He shook the package, but could hear nothing inside it. He sniffed at the parcel, but it smelled of nothing.

'I don't understand what it could be,' he said to himself. 'I don't understand why I can't see inside it. I don't see what harm it could do to have one little look. Perhaps if I just eased aside the string... and carefully lifted this corner...' As the farmer was saying the words, his fingers were poking very gently into the package. But there was nothing to see. He pulled the string away and slowly folded back the paper. Still nothing. He opened the package properly, and saw a tiny pinch of grey powder.

'Well!' he said. 'All that secrecy, and it's only a bit of mouldy old powder.' But as the daylight touched the powder, it puffed away into the air with a strange sighing sound, and the farmer felt suddenly very sad.

He remembered the words of the great rabbit – 'A little bit of immortality, a little bit of everlasting life', and he knew he had just released all kinds of illnesses and deaths into the world, because he could not keep his promise.

The theme of curiosity and/or failure to keep a promise resulting in disaster, is found throughout world literature. The story is found in Zambian legend, where a nomad, seeking to settle down, asks God for seeds. God sends seeds with messengers, but instructs that one packet must never be opened. The messengers disobey, releasing death into the world.

cf. The Greek myth 'Pandora's box', in which a girl is given a box, full of the world's ills, which she is told not to open. Curiosity gets the better of her, she opens the box and releases illness, disease and unhappiness, but also hope, into the world.

See also The Biblical story of Adam and Eve, in which humankind discovers evil because of woman's curiosity and disobedience.

Anansi tries to trick God   *Conceit*
adapted from West African fable

Once upon a time, shortly after Anansi the spider had been made God's chief helper, he started to become very big-headed. He started to boast about how important he was. He told everyone that he was God's most important animal. He told the whole world that no-one could possibly manage without him. And then he began to say that he was even more important than God himself.

At first God took no notice. After all, he was very tolerant and not easily made angry. But the more Anansi boasted, the more irritated God became, until at last his anger exploded.

'Come and see me,' God called. 'I want words with you.'

Anansi went.

'You say you are as important, as clever, as powerful as me? Then prove it!' said God. 'Go and find something for me. But I'm not going to tell you what it is. Find out for yourself!'

Anansi began to search for the 'something' that God wanted, but since he didn't know what it was, he didn't know where to look. Then he had an idea. If he pretended to be someone else, he could perhaps trick God into saying what it was he wanted Anansi to bring him.

Anansi called all the birds together, and asked every one of them to give him a feather. Then he made all the feathers into a splendid shimmering cloak. He put the cloak on and climbed into the branch of a tree. Then he waited to be noticed.

'Who is that bird?' called God. 'I've never seen it before. What is its name?' But no-one was able to tell God the name of the bird in the beautiful coloured feathers.

'Bring the elephant to me,' said God. 'He knows all the creatures. He will be able to tell me who the bird is.'

The elephant came to see God. 'I'm sorry,' he said. 'I don't know its name, but Anansi will know. Why don't you ask him?'

'I can't ask Anansi,' said God. 'He is not here. I have sent him on an errand.'

The people asked God where he had sent Anansi.

'I have sent him to find something,' said God. 'He was boasting that he is as clever as me, so I have sent him to find something that is impossible to find, even if Anansi knew what it was. I have sent him to find the sun and the moon, but he doesn't know what he's looking for.'

Anansi, in his tree, wrapped in his wonderful cloak of feathers, listened to the voice of God, and smiled. He thought he had tricked God.

Later, when the people and God had all gone home, Anansi threw off the shining feather cloak, and went to find the sun and the moon. He caught them and put them in a bag, then went to find God.

'I've brought you something,' he said to God.

'Oh yes?' said God. 'And what have you brought?'

'Look!' said Anansi, and he pulled out the moon from his bag. God looked a bit surprised, then a little worried.

'Anansi, I hope you haven't got the sun in that bag as well. You haven't, have you? You don't understand its power. Anansi, don't let it out of the bag. Anansi, NO!'

But God's warning was too late. Anansi pulled out the sun from his bag. Straightaway, the power of the sun's light blinded everyone who was watching. Its burning light set fire to everything that was near. God threw the sun into the sky before it could do any more damage.

'I'm sorry,' said Anansi. 'I didn't know it was so strong. I didn't know it would blind people or burn things. I'm sorry I boasted and said I was as important as you. I won't do it again, I promise.'

And, for a while at least, Anansi kept his word.

There are many stories of Anansi in African mythology. Anansi (he becomes the Annancy of American fable) is God's chief official, although in the earliest stories he has no name. Anansi is the cleverest animal and is capable of trickery and deceit.

Further reading

The Primal Societies section of *A Handbook of Living Religions* edited by John R Hinnells (Penguin 1984)

The Primal Religions section of *A Handbook of the World's Religions* (Lion 1982)

The Primitive Religion entry in the *Encyclopaedia Britannica*

Religions of Africa N.Q. King (Harper & Row 1970)

The Faber Book of North American Legends edited by Virginia Haviland (Faber & Faber 1979)

Pears Encyclopaedia of Myths and Legends Oceania and Australia, The Americas Sheila Savill (Pelham Books 1978)

African Mythology Geoffrey Parrinder (Newnes Books 1982)

Sikhism

Sikhism is the youngest of the world's major religions, and began with the birth of the first Guru, Guru Nanak, in the Punjab region of India, in 1469 CE.

The Punjab became the homeland and kingdom of the Sikhs, but in 1849 it was taken by the British, as they fought to rule India. The first noticeable migrations of Sikhs occurred in the mid to late 19th century, and were mainly to countries under British rule. Many Sikhs had enlisted in the British army and after their period of active service remained in the countries in which they had last served.

In 1947 the Punjab was divided between India and Pakistan, as India was partitioned. After partition, many Sikhs found themselves homeless and moved from their Punjab homeland to other parts of India. The Sikhs now found themselves dispersed world wide, and throughout India itself.

A small number of Sikhs came to Britain before the First World War, but most came from India or East Africa at the same time as Hindus and Muslims. During the 1950s immigrants filled job vacancies, especially in the textile industries, which could not be filled by native Britons. Britain's need for workers coincided with the closing of the traditional host countries to migrants.

It is believed that there are some 12 million Sikhs living in India (just under 2% of the total population), and that the largest number of Sikhs living outside India is Britain's 250,000.

Sikhism began with the ten great teachers, the first of whom was Guru Nanak (the word 'Guru' means teacher). The title Guru is given to the ten human teachers of Sikhism, and to the Sikh holy book.

Guru Nanak's universally applicable spiritual teaching became known as Sikhism, from the word 'Sikh' – to learn. Guru Nanak travelled extensively with his message of humility, love, peace, service, submission to God, and truth. He visited Hindu and Moslem holy places and taught that the way to God was not through ritual and ceremony, that enlightenment was more important than redemption. Nanak's vision encompassed all races, all countries and all times.

'Know the whole human species as one,' Guru Gobind Singh was later to say.

Guru Nanak's message was carried on by nine subsequent Gurus. The sayings and hymns of them all were incorporated into a holy book, first known as the Adi Granth, and later as the Guru Granth Sahib. This book is considered the 11th Guru, is afforded the respect that a human Guru would be given, and forms the scriptures of the Sikh religion.

The Guru Granth Sahib is unique in scriptures in that

- It was written during the lifetimes of the Gurus. (Most other scriptures were written after the death of the founder. For example, the Hindu Bhagwad Gita was written at least 1000 years after Krishna.)
- It includes writings of people not of the Sikh faith. It contains Hindu and Moslem hymns.
- It is written entirely in poetry and music. Each hymn is preceded by instruction for its musical rhythm.
- It contains imagery of everyday life, used to explain better the profound thoughts expressed within it.
- It is free from dogma.

The basic beliefs of Sikhism are summed up in the Mool Mantra, the first hymn which was composed by Guru Nanak. It appears at the beginning of every chapter in the Guru Granth Sahib.

> There is only one God
> His name is Truth
> He is the creator of all things
> He is fearless and without hate
> He is without form and is eternal
> He is beyond birth and death
> He is self-enlightened
> He is known by the grace of the Guru.

Sikhs live according to rules laid down by the ten Gurus. They include:

- the belief in one God who is omnipresent and the creator of everything
- the need to earn a living by honest means, and to share with others
- that alcohol, tobacco and drugs – except for medicinal use – should not be taken
- that all people are equal.

The ten human Gurus are:

Guru Nanak (1469 – 1539) Born a Hindu. Opposed asceticism.

Guru Angad (1539 – 1552) Consolidated the community. Gathered together the hymns of Guru Nanak.

Guru Amar Das (1552 – 1574) Assembled Sikhs at his village three times a year, at the times of the Hindu festivals. Declared that Sikhs must decide between following the Guru or observing Hindu rituals.

Guru Ram Das (1574 – 1581) Began the building of Amritsar as a place of pilgrimage and worship.

Guru Arjan (1581 – 1606) Completed Amritsar. Collected together the hymns of the four previous Gurus and produced the first version of the Sikh scriptures, the Adi Granth. He died in captivity and became the first martyr Guru of the Sikhs.

Guru Hargobind (1606 – 1644) A hunter and a warrior. He formed the Sikh army.

Guru Har Rai (1644 – 1661) Spent 17 largely uneventful years as leader.

Guru Har Krishan (1661 – 1664) The youngest Guru. He succeeded his predecessor at the age of five, but died of smallpox at the age of eight.

Guru Tegh Bahadur (1664 – 1675) The youngest son of Guru Hargobind. He composed hymns and fought as a soldier against the Mughal rule. He died a martyr's death in Delhi.

Guru Gobind Singh (1675 – 1708) Revised the Adi Granth and installed it as the last Guru, thence known as the Guru Granth Sahib. He founded the Khalsa, the brotherhood of the Sikhs, in 1669. The aim of this was the defence of religious freedom.

The men and women who joined the Khalsa (meaning pure or dedicated ones), were given the name Singh (lion) or Kaur (princess), respectively. The men adopted a distinctive uniform, known as the five Ks. They are

- kesh – the uncut hair
- kanga – the comb
- kara – the steel wrist band
- kirpan – the sword
- kaccha – the shorts.

The stories in this section of *Share Our World* are taken mainly from the *Janam-sakhis*, a collection of biographical (or more correctly hagiographical) accounts of the life of Guru Nanak. They cover the story of his life and journeys, from his birth to his death. The stories illustrate many of Guru Nanak's teachings, and although they are of much lesser importance than the stories in the Guru Granth Sahib, they are nevertheless still influential amongst Sikhs.

Guru Nanak and the tree's shadow
adapted from the Janam-sakhis

God's care/caring for others

When Guru Nanak was a small boy in India, it was his job to look after the family's buffalo. Each day he had to take the buffalo to fields where they could graze. Each day he took them somewhere different so that they could find new fresh green grass to eat. Each day he had to make sure the buffalo had water to drink, and shade to shelter in from the hot sun.

Nanak liked his job. He liked the gentleness of the buffalo. He liked being responsible for them and taking care of them. He especially liked it when there were young, newly-born buffalo to look after. But best of all, Nanak liked the fact that his job gave him time to sit and think. Nanak liked thinking. He liked dreaming. He liked to think of God and of all the wonderful things in the world that God had created.

One day when Nanak had settled the buffalo in a field to graze, and checked that they had clean fresh water to drink, he settled down in the shade of a tree to sit, and think, and dream. The day was very hot and the sun was high overhead. Soon Nanak began to feel sleepy. He settled down more comfortably on the cool green grassy patch under the tree's canopy, and soon he was fast asleep.

He slept for a long time, lying quite still in the shadow of the branches. The sun slowly continued its journey across the clear sky. Gradually, bit by bit, the patch of shadow that Nanak slept in moved across the grass. Slowly, bit by bit, Nanak was uncovered by the shadow and was left lying in the hot glare of the Indian sun. Soon the fierce sun would make his skin hot and red, and he would be burned. Soon he would have sunstroke. Soon he might die because of exposure to the sun.

Nanak slept on. The air was hot and dry and still. The only sound to be heard was the humming and droning of insects as they searched for nectar. The grass smelt warm and sweet as it shrivelled and dried in the sun. Nanak slept on. There was no-one nearby to wake him; to warn him of the danger he was in.

Suddenly there was a rustling and a stirring of leaves and branches high in the tree's canopy. Branches shifted and leaves spread until they were rearranged so that their shadow fell again on the sleeping boy. Nanak was safe for the time being.

The sun continued its journey across the sky. As it travelled in its circle round the earth, it dropped lower in the sky, and its rays lit up places that had earlier been in shadow. The shadows lengthened and changed, moving steadily across the land. But the tree's shadow stayed still. It changed neither shape nor length. It protected Nanak as he slept.

Towards evening, on his way home, the village landlord was astonished to see Nanak lying fast asleep in a cool safe patch of shade, where no shade should have been. All the other shadows had swung round as the day had moved on, but the tree's shadow had stayed still. Unmoving. Immobile. To protect Nanak.

'I've never seen anything like it,' said the landlord. 'The child would have surely died in the sun if the tree had not somehow made its shadow stay still. He must be a very special boy.'

Guru Nanak and the murderer   *Forgiveness/greed*
adapted from the Janam-sakhis

Guru Nanak went travelling with his friend Mardana. Everywhere he went he gave people the same message – to be kind and honest with each other, to live peacefully, and to serve God.

One day Nanak and Mardana came to a big house in the country, owned by a man called Sheikh Sajjan. Sajjan seemed to be kind and helpful.

'Come in,' he said when he saw the travellers. 'Come in and have something to eat and drink. You must be tired after your journey. Have you much further to go?'

'We have some distance still to go', said Nanak, 'But we would like to rest here for a while.'

'You are very welcome to stay here as long as you want,' said Sajjan. 'You must make yourselves at home. My house is yours for as long as you want to stay.'

'Thank you. You are very kind,' said Nanak. But something in Sajjan's voice made Nanak wonder if he was really as generous as he seemed.

Nanak and Mardana were shown around Sajjan's house. It was very big and grand and comfortable. It had a large dining room and huge bedrooms. The garden was beautiful and it had a deep round well in the middle of it. There was a temple and a Mosque in the garden so that Hindu and Moslem travellers could worship their God.

'It's lovely,' said Mardana. 'How lucky you are to live here.'

'Yes,' said Sajjan. 'And you can share it all with me, whilst you are here. Now, come and have something to eat.'

Nanak and Mardana were taken to the dining room, and shown a magnificent table. It was laden with delicious foods. They started to eat. Sajjan watched them. He smiled to himself. Soon he would take them for another walk in the garden. He would lead them past the well. It would be easy to push them in. They would quickly die. They would drown in the deep water at the bottom. The sides were too steep for them to climb out. He had killed lots of men that way. Killed them then stolen their money and belongings. Sajjan had become rich on the money of his murdered guests.

Soon Nanak and Mardana had finished their meal.

'What would you like to do now?' asked Sajjan. 'Why don't we go for a walk in the garden again, before you go to sleep?' and he smiled to himself again at the thought of the long sleep which the travellers would soon have.

'I think it would be nice to sit quietly for a while,' said Guru Nanak. 'I think it would be peaceful to sit and think. Or perhaps listen to a story. Or perhaps sing a hymn.'

'Very well,' agreed Sajjan. After all, he didn't mind if he waited a little while before killing the two men. Another hour wouldn't make any difference.

Nanak began to sing. He sang a peaceful hymn, that told of the goodness of God. He sang a song as quiet as a lullaby, that told of the kindness of God. He sang a gentle hymn that told of God's strength. And then he sang a song that told of a man who wanted to steal from others. A man who wanted to harm others. A man who wanted to kill others. And Sajjan recognised himself.

Suddenly he felt ashamed of all the wrong things he had done. He knelt at Guru Nanak's feet and asked for his forgiveness.

'I'm sorry. I've done wrong. Please forgive me,' he said.

'You can be forgiven,' said Guru Nanak. 'But only on condition that you try to put right all the wrong things you have done. Only on condition that you repay everything you have ever stolen. Only on condition that you help others, to try to compensate for those people you have killed.'

Sajjan agreed to try to put right the things he had done wrong in the past, and he promised to lead a better life in the future.

cf. 'The Robber', page 72, in which a thief changes his lifestyle in response to the kindness he is shown by another. Although the plot of the two stories is different, the end result, achieved through non-violence, is the same.

Guru Nanak and the bowl of milk   *Greed/selfishness/tolerance/forgiveness*
adapted from the Janam-sakhis

Guru Nanak and his friend Mardana had travelled a long way. They were tired and hungry as they walked along the road towards the city of Multan.

'We'll soon be there,' said Mardana. 'I expect the people will be kind and friendly, and they'll help us find something to eat, and somewhere to stay.'

But the people of Multan had already spotted the travellers, and they were not intending being kind, or friendly, or helpful. In fact they had every intention of sending the visitors away as soon as possible.

You see, there were many priests and holy men living in the city at that time. They gave help and advice to people who came to see them, and in return, the people gave them money or gifts. The priests and holy men had grown rich and fat and contented on the profits they had made. They didn't want any more holy men in their city. When they saw Guru Nanak and Mardana coming towards them they said 'We don't want any more people here. We must get rid of them.

We don't want newcomers.'

They all gathered together near the gate of the city, to decide what to do.

'We could frighten them away,' said one.

'We could throw stones at them,' said another.

'We could shout at them,' said someone.

'We could tell them to go on to the next town,' said someone else. 'We could say that our city is full.'

'We could just be honest and tell them that we don't want them here,' someone said.

'No!' said one of the priests. 'We can't do any of those things. It isn't polite. We cannot be rude to them, even if we don't want them here. No. We must think of a better way. A clever way. A way that will make it clear that we don't want them here, without actually telling them so.'

The priests and holy men thought in silence for a long time. Then one of them spoke again.

'We'll wait until they're almost here, then we'll send them a bowl of milk. But the bowl must be so full that there isn't space for a single drop more. Guru Nanak and his friend will realise that our city is so full, that there isn't space for even one more person.'

'That's a very clever idea,' said the other priests and holy men. 'Guru Nanak is a clever man. He will understand the message.'

The priests waited until Guru Nanak and Mardana were almost at the city gate. They they called for a servant. They told the servant to get a bowl of milk.

'It must be full to the brim,' they said to him. 'It must be impossible to get even one more drop into the bowl.'

The servant did as he was asked. He carried the bowl carefully, steadily, so as not to spill a single drop of milk. He walked up to Guru Nanak and Mardana and offered them the bowl.

'Look,' said Mardana. 'They are welcoming us with a drink. That's kind, isn't it.'

'No,' said Guru Nanak, gently. 'This is not a gift of welcome. This is a message telling us not to come to their city. See how full the bowl is. See how there is not space for even one more drop of milk. They are telling us there is no room here for us. But I have a message for them. I want to tell them that there is always space in the world for love and compassion. There is always space for goodness and kindness.' And Guru Nanak picked a beautiful jasmine flower from a bush that was growing near the gate of the city.

He carefully floated the flower on top of the milk. It rested on the creamy liquid, delicately scenting it, but it did not make the milk spill over the sides of the bowl. There was room in the bowl for all the milk *and* the jasmine flower.

'Take this bowl of milk back to the priests and holy men,' said Guru Nanak to the servant. 'They will understand the message.'

The servant again did as he was asked. He walked carefully, slowly, so as not to spill a single drop of the milk.

'Look,' said the priests and holy men, when they saw what Guru Nanak had done. 'He is telling us that the bowl had room for something else, even though it seemed to be full. He is saying that there is room for him in our city. He is giving us the message that there should be room in our hearts for other people.'

And the priests and holy men of Multan felt ashamed that they had tried to turn Guru Nanak away. They felt ashamed of their selfishness and greed. They went to greet Guru Nanak and Mardana, and welcomed them to their city.

The two villages   *Generosity/caring for others/selfishness*
adapted from the Janam-sakhis

When Guru Nanak and his friend Mardana were on their travels, they came to a pleasant-looking village.

'This looks like a good place to stop and rest,' said Mardana. 'I think we'll be able to find somewhere here to stay for a while.'

The two friends followed the road leading directly into the village, and came to the first house. They knocked on the door.

'Could you tell us where we might find the inn, please?' they asked.

'There's nowhere here to stay,' answered a surly-looking man. 'Visitors are not welcome in these parts,' and he slammed the door in their faces.

Guru Nanak and Mardana looked at each other.

'Perhaps he was just in a bad mood,' said Mardana. 'Let's try another house.'

They walked on until they came to the next house, and they knocked on the door.

'Could you please tell us where we might find an inn, or somewhere to stay for the night?' they asked.

'No!' said the woman who answered the door. 'There's nowhere like that here,' and she banged the door shut.

'Well!' said Mardana. 'It's not a very friendly place is it?' They tried several more houses, but always the answer was the same. 'We don't want you here. We don't like visitors. Go away.'

Guru Nanak and Mardana decided that the only thing to do was to walk on to the next village, in the hope that they met with better luck there. If not, they would have no choice but to sleep out in the open that night.

After an hour's trudging, they approached the first house of the next village. A man saw them coming.

'Hello,' he said. 'You look thirsty, not to mention tired and hungry. Would you like a cool drink of water. I can bring it to you outside now.'

'Thank you,' said the travellers.

The man hurried indoors and came out with two cups of cool clear clean water. It was fresh and delicious. The man talked to them while they drank.

Who were they and where were they going? Why had they come this way? Did they want somewhere to stop for the night? He had a friend who ran an inn. He would be pleased to put them up. He served good meals, at good fair prices. Would the travellers like him to contact his friend and arrange something?

All the time that they were talking together, other people were walking along the road, on their way home or wherever, and every time someone passed, they said 'Good evening', 'Hello' or 'Good day'. People were friendly and helpful, and it seemed that everyone wanted the two travellers to be happy during their stay in the village. Everyone wanted them to be comfortable, to feel welcome, and to think well of the village and its people.

Guru Nanak and Mardana spent a happy few hours in the company of the villagers, and a comfortable night in the inn.

The next day they left to continue their travels.

'I hope that village is uprooted, and its people scattered,' said Guru Nanak, as they walked away.

'That seems unfair,' said Mardana. 'Why should you wish that they be uprooted and scattered. Surely it would be fairer if you wished the people from the *other* village to be uprooted and scattered. After all, they were unfriendly and unhelpful. The people in *this* village were kind and generous. Surely it's fairer if they stay in their village and live peaceful undisturbed lives?'

'No,' said Guru Nanak. 'If the people in the selfish village became scattered throughout the world, they would make everyone else selfish too. But if the people in the kind village spread themselves throughout the world, they will help make the world a better place, because they will spread their kindness and their friendliness and their generosity. I'd like all the kind and friendly people in the world to help everyone else to be kind and friendly too.'

'Yes,' said Mardana. 'I understand.'

Guru Nanak and the wealthy man   *Greed/conceit*
adapted from the Janam-sakhis

When Guru Nanak went travelling, he once visited the city of Lahore, where there lived a very wealthy man. His name was Duni Chand and he was the richest person for miles around.

Duni Chand had a huge and beautiful palace. He had magnificent gardens, fine ornaments, rare jewels, wonderful clothes, dozens of servants, lots of animals, plenty of friends, everything in fact that anyone could want. And Duni Chand was proud of his wealth.

He liked everyone to know how rich he was. He liked to show off about it. He liked to get richer and richer every year, so that he could boast about it. He even had flags flying outside his palace to show the people who passed by how much money he had. Each flag represented ten thousand gold coins, and at the time of

Guru Nanak's visit, there were seven flags flying outside the palace.

When Duni Chand heard that Guru Nanak was coming to Lahore, he hurriedly made arrangements to hold a special banquet in his honour. After all, as the richest man in Lahore, it was the least he could do. The people would expect it.

He ordered the very best and most exotic foods. He arranged for musicians to come and play new music; he planned to have wonderful flowers brought into the palace. At last everything was ready and the banquet was ready to start. The guests had all arrived. They were just waiting for the guest of honour – Guru Nanak.

He came. He looked at the marble palace decorated with silver and gold. He gazed at the seven flags flying outside. He saw the lovely flowers and the wonderful dining room. He sat down at the table laden with delicious foods. The banquet began. It was a great success and everyone said it was the best banquet they had ever attended.

After the meal, Duni Chand turned to Guru Nanak and said,

'I am a very rich man. I will buy you anything you want. What do you want to have?' All the guests fell quiet as they waited to hear what Guru Nanak would say.

For a long time he said nothing. Then he reached in to his pocket and pulled out a small slim leather case. He opened the case and took out a tiny silver needle.

'I would like you to save this for me,' he said. 'I would like to save it, and give it to me when we meet again in the next life.' Then Guru Nanak thanked Duni Chand for the meal, and left his house.

'Look at that,' boasted Duni Chand to his wife and his friends and guests. 'He's given me this to save for him. He has entrusted it to *me*. What a responsibility! What a job! How wonderful that he's asked *me* to do it!'

'You foolish man,' scoffed his wife. 'You think you've been given a special job, but how do you think you're going to give anyone anything in the *next* life. You can't take anything with you to the next life when you die.'

Duni Chand listened to what his wife said, and knew she was right. What then had Guru Nanak meant? Why had he given him the small silver needle? 'I must go and find him, and ask him what he meant by it,' said Duni Chand, and he too left the house.

He caught up easily with Guru Nanak.

'I don't understand,' he said. 'What are you trying to tell me? Why have you given me this needle?'

'If you cannot take this needle with you into the next life,' said Guru Nanak. 'Then how are you going to take all your wealth with you? How are you going to take the flags that fly outside your palace with you?'

'I am not,' said Duni Chand, indignantly.

'Then why are you hoarding all that wealth?' asked Guru Nanak. 'Why are you keeping it all to yourself and showing off about it. Why don't you share it with others, and put it to some good use during your time on earth? You will be remembered then by your good deeds, and not as the man who was rich but did nothing with his riches. Think about it.'

Duni Chand did think about it. He went home and talked to his wife about the conversation he'd had with Guru Nanak. And from that day on, Duni Chand tried to use his wealth to help other people. He tried to share what he had with others, and he felt ashamed of the times when he had boasted about how rich he was.

cf The Biblical story of the rich man who asked Jesus how he could achieve eternal life. Jesus answered 'It is much harder for a rich person to enter the Kingdom of God than for a camel to go through the eye of a needle' (Matthew 19:24). The story is also found in Mark 10:17-31 and Luke 18:18-30.

Guru Nanak visits Mecca   *God is everywhere*
adapted from the Janam-sakhis

One day Guru Nanak and his friend Mardana travelled to the city of Mecca. Mecca is the holy city of Muslim people, and Muslims from all over the world come to pray in the holy mosque in Mecca. Mardana and Guru Nanak entered the mosque. There were many people there. Some were praying, others were sitting quietly, thinking, and some were walking round the Ka'bah – the holy shrine in the centre of the mosque.

Guru Nanak and Mardana were tired. They had come a long way. They sat down on the ground and were soon both fast asleep.

Suddenly, the mullah – the teacher – came hurrying over to them. He kicked Guru Nanak's feet, and shouted at him.

'What do you think you're doing? How dare you lie down here with your feet pointing to the Ka'bah. Don't you know that it is rude to point your feet at the holy shrine? People's feet are unclean. Look at yours. They have been walking on the dusty roads. Move your feet away from the Ka'bah? Show some respect!' And the mullah kicked Guru Nanak's legs again.

Guru Nanak looked at the mullah and said, 'I'm sorry I've upset you. It's just that we were so tired when we got here, we just fell asleep. But please, if my feet offend you, turn them to where there is no house of God.'

The mullah was so angry with Guru Nanak, he grabbed hold of his legs and swung them round so that they were pointing in the opposite direction. But when he stood up again, the mullah saw with astonishment that the Ka'bah had changed direction too. Guru Nanak's feet were still pointing to it. And to make matters worse, several people were now standing around watching this strange happening.

The mullah grabbed hold of Guru Nanak's legs again. He pulled them round to point in a different direction. The Ka'bah moved to follow them. Some more people came to watch. There was quite a crowd now.

The mullah stood up straight and tall, and thought. This needs a systematic approach, he decided. Without saying a word, he picked up Guru Nanak's legs once more, and turned them so that they pointed towards the north. The Ka'bah moved to the north. He held Guru Nanak's legs again and pulled them round so they were pointing south. The Ka'bah moved to the south. In exasperation he swung Guru Nanak's legs to the east. The Ka'bah moved east. And in desperation he pushed Guru Nanak's legs to point west. The Ka'bah moved to the west.

'I just don't understand it,' the mullah cried. 'Nothing like this has ever happened before.' The crowd standing around agreed that the Ka'bah never normally moved or changed position. People started to look anxious and worried, they didn't understand this strange occurrence. What was happening? What did it mean?

'It means', said Guru Nanak, 'That God is not in just one place. He is not to be found in one building, or one city, or one country. God is everywhere. He lives in each and every one of us. We can find him wherever we look. We can speak to him wherever we are. We can hear him whenever we listen.

'I am sorry if I upset you by not keeping the rules of the mosque, but it is important to me that you understand that God is everywhere.'

Guru Nanak then started to sing a beautiful song about God. Mardana joined in the singing, and the rest of the people listened, until they too were able to join in.

The Travellers in the wilderness *Appearances can be deceptive/cheerfulness in adversity/think for yourself/doing your best/ keeping your word/loyalty*

adapted from the Janam-sakhis

Guru Nanak and Mardana had travelled through towns, cities and villages. But now they came to a wilderness, a great expanse of barren land strewn with rocks and boulders, where nothing seemed to be alive. As far as they could see, there was deserted landscape. No houses. No people. No comfort. No life. Nothing. The whole place had a strange and empty feel to it, as though it belonged to no-one, and no-one belonged to it.

Guru Nanak and Mardana sat down on the ground to rest.

Suddenly, to Mardana's terror, the day became black as night. Thunder rolled and great flashes of lightning ripped the sky apart. Wind howled round the boulders behind which the travellers hid; wind so fierce that the rocks and earth shook with the strength of it. Mardana trembled, as flames crackled and snapped in the distance. He could see smoke curling and writhing on the horizon. Then he saw Kaliyug, the Evil One.

Kaliyug seemed as big as a giant; his head in the clouds and his feet on the ground. Mardana, in his fear, cowered against the boulder, but saw Guru Nanak stand, firm and tall and sure, without fear, as though he were simply going to greet a visitor.

Kaliyug, the Evil One, approached, but the nearer he came the smaller he grew, until by the time he reached the friends, he was only the size of a man. Guru Nanak spoke to him politely.

'We meet at last,' said Kaliyug. 'Now, I have a deal to make with you. Come with me. Come and be with me and I will give you wonderful riches. I will give you a beautiful palace with walls of silver and gold and floors of marble. You will want for nothing if you come and follow me.'

'No thank you,' said Guru Nanak. 'I have promised that I will follow only God and goodness. I will not follow your evil ways, Kaliyug.'

'You don't know what you're missing,' went on Kaliyug. 'Come and follow me and I will look after your every need. I will give you jewels and marvellous clothes. I will give you friends and people around you who will worship you. All you have to do is follow me.'

'No!' said Guru Nanak. 'I don't want your costly things. I want to lead a good life and help my fellow man. I have given my word that I will follow only God. I will not follow you, Evil One.'

'But I have powers that would astound you ' said Kaliyug. 'If you come with me and be with me, I will give you the power to work miracles. Think how wonderful that would be. Think how people would look up to you if you could do that. Come on, give it some thought. You know you'd like to be able to work miracles. Come with me and you'll be able to.'

'No!' said Guru Nanak, remaining calm and quiet. 'I have already told you. I will serve only God and goodness. I will not follow you.'

'Then what about being KING?' persisted Kaliyug. 'I have the power to be able to make you a king. I can make you king of all you survey. Come on. All you have to do is agree to follow me and I will make you a king.'

'No!' said Guru Nanak. 'Whatever you say, whatever you offer me will not make me change my mind. I will not follow you, or serve you, or even take any notice of you. You stand for evil and wickedness and I will have nothing to do with it. I have given my word that I will only follow God, and I intend to keep my word. Now, please go away and leave me alone.'

Kaliyug realised that he was never going to persuade Guru Nanak to turn his back on God. He realised that he was speaking to a truly good man.

'Have pity on me,' he said to Guru Nanak. 'I ask you to forgive me.'

'It is for God to forgive you,' answered Guru Nanak. 'He will do that if you give up your evil ways and live a life of goodness. Can you do that?'

But Kaliyug had already left and gave no answer.

It remained to be seen in the future what he would do.

cf. The Biblical story of Jesus in the wilderness, when he is tempted by the devil but refuses to turn away from God (Matthew 4:1-11, Mark 1:12-13 and Luke 4:1-13).

Guru Nanak at the mosque   *Insincerity/dishonesty*
adapted from the Janam-sakhis

One day Guru Nanak visited the mosque. He talked to some people and one of them asked, 'Are you a Hindu or a Muslim?'

'I am not a Hindu and I am not a Muslim either,' answered Guru Nanak. 'People are human beings and God lives in them all. I do not recognise any difference between them.'

When Guru Nanak said this, the Muslim teacher became angry, because he thought that Guru Nanak was not showing respect to the Muslims. But, before he had time to question Guru Nanak any further, the bell sounded to call the people to prayer.

Everyone went inside the mosque. Nanak, and the teacher, and a man called Daulat Khan, who was the governor of the area, went inside together.

Everything was quiet and still, as the people began their prayers. Everyone was thinking about God and concentrating on their thoughts. Suddenly, Guru Nanak stopped praying and looked at the teacher and at Daulat Khan. Then he laughed. The people were furious. After the prayers they came to ask Guru Nanak what he meant by his disgraceful behaviour.

'We were having a conversation about you not showing respect, before we even went in to prayers,' shouted the teacher angrily. 'And now you have shown even more disrespect by laughing in the middle of them. Your behaviour is disgraceful. Explain yourself!'

'You were not fit to join us in the mosque,' said Daulat Khan. 'You should never have come. How could you show us up like that. We were saying our prayers in the way we have been taught, and you dared to laugh. Why?'

'It is you who were not fit to be saying prayers,' said Guru Nanak.

'How dare you speak to us like that,' the two men shouted.

'Listen to me,' answered Guru Nanak. 'You tell me that you were praying in the way you should. I say you were not. You, Daulat Khan, were in fact thinking about some horses your servant is buying for you. Is that not right?'

Daulat Khan looked away. He knew that Guru Nanak spoke the truth. He had been thinking about the horses instead of concentrating on his prayers.

'And you,' said Guru Nanak to the teacher. 'You were also not concentrating on your prayers. You were worried about the new foal in your field. You have forgotten to tether him haven't you? You have forgotten to tie him up safely, and you are worried that he might stray to the far side of your field where there is a deep well. Am I not speaking the truth?'

The teacher was speechless. Guru Nanak knew what he had been thinking. He was right. The teacher had not been praying to God, but had been wondering whether the new foal was all right.

'You see,' said Guru Nanak. 'It is all very well for you to accuse me of not praying properly. But you should first make sure that you are without blame.'

'You are right,' said Daulat Khan to Guru Nanak. 'We were wrong to accuse you when we ourselves were in the wrong. Will you please forgive us. I feel so ashamed of my behaviour, that I give you, here and now, all my money and my possessions. You can use what is mine to help the poor. I am truly sorry.' And immediately Daulat Khan gave away the money and jewels he had with him. 'You can have the rest as soon as I go home,' he said.

The money was given to the poor over the next few days. But the strangest thing was that later, when Daulat Khan went to his money chest, everything he had given away had somehow been restored to him, and he was able to give it away again.

When Guru Nanak saw that Daulat Khan and the teacher were trying to help others, he continued on his travels, with Mardana, his friend.

An invitation to a meal   *Greed/honesty/appearances can be deceptive*
adapted from the Janam-sakhis

Lalo lived in a town called Eminabad. He was a carpenter, and spent every day working with wood. Sometimes he made chairs or tables, sometimes he made wooden toys, sometimes he repaired wooden things for people, but always he was busy. Lalo was a good craftsman. He was hardworking, honest and cheerful. He always did his best work, whether it was for a friend, or a customer he didn't know. Yet despite all his hard work, Lalo was poor.

One day Guru Nanak and his friend Mardana travelled to Eminabad. They went to stay at Lalo's house. He was pleased to see them and said they could stay as long as they wanted.

'I haven't much', he said, 'But whatever I have is yours to share.' Guru Nanak and Mardana thanked Lalo and said they would like to stay for a few days.

Now it happened that while they were there, a rich man in the neighbourhood decided to hold a banquet. His name was Malak Bhago and he was extremely wealthy. Malak Bhago sent out invitations to all the important people of Eminabad. He didn't, of course, send an invitation to Lalo, because he was, after all, only a poor carpenter. No, Malak Bhago only sent invitations to the eminent people – the important people.

He invited the businessmen, the bankers, the governor, the viceroy, and all the holy men of the town. Then Malak Bhago heard that Guru Nanak was in town. He must be invited. He must come. He must be the guest of honour.

Malak Bhago sent an invitation to Guru Nanak at Lalo's house.

'Please come to dinner at seven o'clock' it read. 'RSVP'.

Guru Nanak replied straight away.

'I am sorry I am unable to come,' he wrote. 'But I will be having dinner with my friend Lalo this evening. Thank you.'

When Malak Bhago read the reply he was furious. How dare Guru Nanak turn down his invitation? No-one turned down invitations to dine with the great Malak Bhago. Whatever was Nanak thinking of? Anyway, what was so special about having dinner with Lalo? He was only an ordinary carpenter, a workman, a common sort of person. He wouldn't be preparing delicious and rare foods for dinner at *his* house, like Malak Bhago's servants would be doing.

The more Malak Bhago thought about his invitation being turned down, the more angry he became. In the end he decided he must go and speak to Guru Nanak, to find out for himself why he would not come to dine.

Malak Bhago marched through the streets and came to Lalo's house. He knocked on the door.

'Come in,' said Guru Nanak, as though he were not at all surprised to see the great man standing on the doorstep.

'How can I help you?'

'I want to know why you're not coming to my dinner,' demanded Malak Bhago. 'I want to know why you are going to have dinner with this... this... carpenter, instead of me.'

'That's easy to answer,' said Guru Nanak. 'But first, bring me something that we are going to eat tonight.'

'Now?' asked Malak Bhago, puzzled.

'Now!' said Nanak.

Whilst Malak Bhago was away getting some of the delicious fried pastries that would be served at the dinner, Guru Nanak went into Lalo's kitchen and took a vegetable cake that he knew was for the evening meal.

Soon Malak Bhago came back with the delicacies. Guru Nanak took one of the pastries in his hand. In his other hand he picked up Lalo's vegetable cake. Then he held both hands over a tray and squeezed them tightly.

Malak Bhago was astonished to see some drops of milk dripping out of Lalo's vegetable cake, but he was even more surprised to see drops of blood dripping from his own fried pastries.

'What is the meaning of this?' he asked. 'What are you trying to tell me?'

'I am trying to tell you', said Guru Nanak, 'That Lalo's vegetable cake had been made honestly. He has earned an honest day's wage to buy his dinner tonight. But your pastries, they have been paid for with money you have stolen from others. You have not done an honest day's work to pay for tonight's dinner, have you!'

Malak Bhago could not answer because he knew that Nanak's words were true.

'So you see,' went on Guru Nanak, 'I would rather eat with an honest man than a dishonest one, any day. Now, if you'll excuse me, I must go and get ready for the meal. It is almost time to eat.'

Malak Bhago went back to his own house. He cancelled the banquet he had planned for that evening. He knew he had a great deal of thinking to do.

The donkey and the tiger skin   *Appearances can be deceptive/caring for animals/honesty*

adapted from Sikh teaching

Guru Gobind Singh was once riding through the city of Anandpur when he heard the noise of an animal in pain. He stopped to listen, and there it was again. It sounded like a donkey. Guru Gobind Singh followed the sound and came upon the sorry sight of the potter's donkey. It was being forced to carry an extremely heavy load of pots, and was almost collapsing under the weight. To make matters worse, people round about were laughing at the poor animal.

Guru Gobind Singh felt sorry for the donkey, and said to its owner, 'If you halve his load he might do better. Carry on like that and he'll probably die.' The potter grudgingly took some of the pots off the donkey's back, which made his load a little easier to bear, but the people still laughed and jeered at the animal.

The Guru walked away; there was little else he could do. But as he went he thought how differently the people would have reacted if the animal had been a tiger instead of a donkey. And that thought gave the Guru an idea.

He went home and collected a tiger skin that someone had once brought him for a present. It was a full size skin, and would fit the donkey perfectly.

Guru Gobind Singh went back to the potter. He was nowhere to be seen, but the donkey was tethered outside. The Guru quietly led the donkey away, put the tiger skin on its back, then led it back to the market place where he let it go.

At first the donkey was unsure what to do. It had been to the market place many times before, but always in the company of its master, always carrying a heavy load. This time the load was light. Light as a skin in fact. The donkey started to amble down the road. It could see the brightly coloured market stalls up ahead. It could smell the tantalising market smells in its nostrils.

Suddenly, the donkey heard a tremendous shout.

'Help! Tiger! Run! Get out of the way!' And he was astonished to see people scattering in all directions. This was most unusual. People normally took no notice of him. He might as well be invisible most of the time.

Then the donkey saw that not only were the people running away from him, but the cats and dogs, horses and cows, goats and sheep and chickens and ducks were also quickly getting out of the way. The donkey found himself standing all alone in the middle of the market.

He walked across to a fruit stall. He stretched out his neck and took a ripe apple. Delicious. No-one stopped him. He tried another. Then a plum or two.

Next a bun from the bread stall. Tasty. No-one challenged him. No-one said no. The donkey had no idea why he was being allowed to behave like this. He didn't understand why the stallholders were taking no notice of him. He didn't see that the people were hastily meeting behind the safety of some trees.

'What shall we do?' they said.

'That tiger is going to ruin all our produce.'

'It must be stopped.'

'But who is brave enough to face up to a tiger?'

'Someone has to.'

'But who?'

'And how?'

Then someone suggested that they all work together to frighten the tiger back into the jungle.

'If we all rush out together, shouting and waving sticks and banging drums and saucepan lids and anything else that will make a dreadful din, then surely we will frighten it away, and no-one will get hurt.'

'Good idea!'

So the people armed themselves with sticks and lids and drums and whistles and rushed out into the road. The donkey jumped out of its skin and brayed loudly in panic and fear.

'Hee haw. Hee haw. Hee haw.'

The people stood still and stared.

'It's the potter's donkey!' someone said. 'It's not a tiger at all. Look. It was wearing this skin.' And he held up the tiger skin that had fallen to the ground in the crush.

Just then Guru Gobind Singh appeared in the road.

'Yes,' he said. 'A donkey, not a tiger.' He gently stroked the donkey's nose. 'He looked like a tiger. He wore the skin of a tiger. But underneath he was a donkey, with the sound and the actions of a donkey.'

Guru Gobind Singh turned to the crowd. 'Here is a lesson for us all,' he said, 'Let's not try to be something we're not. Let's be brave enough to be ourselves. We are Sikhs. We wear the uniform of Sikhs. Let us be true to that uniform; brave and honest, loyal and true. Let's not be like the donkey in the tiger skin.'

And Guru Gobind Singh quietly led the donkey back to the potter, having taught his people a lesson.

cf. 'The donkey in the lion's skin' by Aesop. In this almost identical tale, the moral is 'do not pretend to be something you are not. If you do, be careful; it's easy to give yourself away.'

The same story is also found in the Jataka Tales – the Sihacamma-Jataka. In this version a merchant puts his donkey to grass in a lion's skin for safety. One day the villagers come with arms, scare the donkey, and in his fright he brays loudly. The angry villagers beat the donkey to death.

Further reading

For teachers
A History of the Sikh People Dr Gopal Singh (World Sikh University Press 1979)
Comparative Religions ed. W. Owen Cole (Blandford Press 1982)
Guru Nanak and the Sikh Religion W.H. McLeod (Oxford University Press 1968)
Sikhism W. Owen Cole and P.S. Sambhi (Ward Lock 1973)
Sikhism and its Indian Context 1469-1708 W. Owen Cole (Darton, Longman & Todd 1984)
Six Religions in the Twentieth Century W. Owen Cole with Peggy Morgan (Hulton Educational 1984)
The B40 Janam Sakhi W.H. McLeod (Amritsar 1980)
The Sikhs: their Religious Beliefs and Practices W. Owen Cole and P.S. Sambhi (Routledge and Kegan Paul 1987)

For children
Guru Nanak and the Sikh Gurus Ranjit Arora (Wayland 1987)
I am a Sikh M. Aggarwal and H.S. Lal (Franklin Watts 1984)
Our Sikh Friends Anne Farncombe (National Christian Education Council 1978)
Sikh Festivals Dr Sukhbir Singh Kapoor (Wayland 1985)
Stories from the Sikh World Rani & Jugnu Singh (Macdonald 1987)
The Living Festivals Series – Guru Nanak's Birthday Margaret Davidson (RMEP 1982)
The Sikh World Daljit Singh & Angela Smith (Macdonald 1985)
Understanding Your Sikh Neighbour P.S. Sambhi (Lutterworth Press 1980)

Useful addresses

Independent Publishing Co. (Soma Books), 38 Kennington Lane, London SE11 4LS
Sikh Missionary Society (UK) 10 Featherstone Road, Southall, Middlesex UB2 5AA

Traditional Western Fables

No collection of fables would be complete without mention of Aesop or La Fontaine. Although these fables are not drawn directly from a religious background, the stories are colourful, and the messages within them are as relevant today as when they were written.

The history of Western fable begins effectively with Aesop, believed to have been a disabled Greek slave who lived in Phrygia between 620 and 560 BCE. (Aesop is also the name of a river in Phrygia, and of a Trojan in the siege of Troy.) Aesopian fables are fables of various dates which were gathered together under Aesop's name.

The earliest surviving collection of Aesop's fables dates from the first century CE. However, some of the tales have been found on Egyptian papyrus, pre-dating Aesop by some 800–1000 years. A large number of the fables have been traced back to Indian sources, especially to the 'Kalilah and Dimnah', known as the *Fables of Bidpai*. This work is reputed to have been an 8th century translation of the Sanskrit Panchatantra into Arabic. Bidpai is believed to be from the Arabic 'Bidbah' meaning wise man. The title Bidpai was applied to the chief scholar at the court of an Indian prince.

Most European writers of fables admit the effect of Aesop on their work. Indeed, La Fontaine (1621–1695), reputed to be the greatest fabulist of modern Europe and one of the most talented writers of the reign of Louis XIV, closely followed the style of Aesop when he wrote his first collection of fables in 1668. It has been said that the first collection was merely Aesop rewritten.

La Fontaine's subsequent work, over the next 25 years, satirized the French court. His animal characters were convincing as animals, but the analogy between them and the courtiers, clergy, lawyers, merchants and peasants which they represented, was clearly apparent. La Fontaine wrote as an observer, rather than as a moralist, but his fables each carry a moral nevertheless.

Fable found a new audience in the middle of the last century, with the advent of literature written specifically for children. The Victorians placed emphasis on utility in children's literature, and liked the didactic fable, which would help teach children to behave in socially acceptable ways. Thus the simpler and more obvious of Aesop's fables found favour and a resurgence of popularity.

At the same time, the writing of literary fables became a serious art form, and many authors used the medium of fable to express themselves. The fable became satire, and moved on from being a simple allegory with a tag line at the end.

Celebrated writers who have used the medium include Hans Anderson, Hilaire Belloc, Lewis Carroll, Kenneth Grahame, Joel Chandler Harris, Franz Kafka, Rudyard Kipling, Beatrix Potter, Antoine Saint-Exupery, Robert Louis Stevenson, James Thurber, JRR Tolkein, Oscar Wilde, and of course George Orwell. Orwell's *Animal Farm* is one of the most celebrated fables of our time, in its blistering allegorical portrayal of Stalinist Russia.

Fable continues today, and echoes the changes in our society, as indeed it has done since its conception. In Spike Milligan's *The White Flag* conflict is ended in atomic destruction. And in Schulz' comic strip *Peanuts* with its messages for the people of our times, we see a direct relationship with the Aesopian tradition dating back two and a half thousand years.

The bee-keeper and the bees
adapted from Aesop

Jumping to conclusions

There was once a man who kept bees. He had several bee hives, called skeps, which were made of cane and grasses, and which looked like large upturned shopping baskets.

The man was a good bee-keeper. He looked after the bees carefully. He always made sure that the skeps were in good repair, that they had not become broken or damaged. He fed the bees with sugar syrup so that they would be able to make plenty of sweet honey, and he never took *all* their honey from them. He took just as much as he needed for his own use and to sell at the market. The rest he left for the bees, who need the honey for the young bees to eat.

One day, a thief came snooping round. He hid in the bushes and watched the bee-keeper. He saw him carefully lift up the edge of the skep and take out a honey comb. He saw the glistening golden honey dripping from the beautiful six-sided cells of the comb. He saw how slowly and gently and carefully the bee-keeper handled the honey combs, so as not to startle and frighten the bees that were still in the hive.

He watched the bee-keeper place six honey combs in a large bowl. He saw him put the bee skeps back in place. And he watched him go back in to his house, to transfer the honey to jars, ready for market.

'Now's my chance,' said the thief to himself. 'He'll be inside for a few minutes. He'll be gone long enough for me to take the rest of the honey. I can sell it and get a good price.'

The thief ran to the skeps. He knocked them to the ground then kicked them over so that the honey combs fell out on to the grass. The bees inside the skeps flew out and buzzed round him angrily, but the thief took no notice and grabbed as many pieces of honey comb as he could stuff into his bag. Then he ran, as fast as he had ever run before, away from the angry stinging bees, away from the broken skeps, and away from the bee-keeper, who was just coming out of his house.

'What?' said the bee-keeper. 'Whatever has happened here? Who has broken my bee hives? I've never seen anything like it. They're all smashed. Where is the rest of the honey? Oh, my poor bees.'

The bee-keeper ran to the broken skeps. They were damaged almost beyond repair. The ground round about was sticky with honey that had spilled from the combs as the thief ran away. The woven sides of the skeps were split apart and the basket-work was torn open. The bees flew aimlessly above the damage.

'It's a good thing that most of the bees are out of the hives just now,' said the bee-keeper. 'It's a good thing that they're away collecting pollen and nectar. It'll give me time to try to mend these skeps before they're back.' And the bee-keeper set about collecting canes and grasses, rushes and raffia to mend the broken skeps.

But the bee-keeper had barely begun when the first of the worker bees returned. They saw others of their family flying angrily round in the air. They saw their skeps, lying broken and damaged on the ground. They saw the pools of wasted honey, drying stickily in the sun. And they saw the bee-keeper in the middle of it all. They saw what had happened... the bee-keeper had destroyed their homes. It must have been him because he was there, standing by the broken skeps.

The bees attacked. They gathered together in a huge dark swarm and swirled through the air towards the bee-keeper. Every second, more and more bees joined the swarm until the sky was black with them. The bee-keeper started to run. It was the first time he had ever felt afraid of his bees, the first time they had ever threatened to attack, the first time he had ever been stung over and over again until he cried out with the pain of it.

When the bee-keeper eventually fell to the ground and lay quite still, the bees left him alone. They turned and headed back to their skeps. Only then did they realise that now there was no-one to rebuild their homes. Only then did they wonder why the man who had always looked after them, should suddenly smash the skeps. Only then did they question whether they had been right to blame him.

But now it was too late.

cf. 'The mongoose and the snake' page 62, in which the same theme is expressed but using a different plot. See also the notes on page 63.

The woodcutter's axe

adapted from Aesop   *Greed/honesty*

There was once a woodcutter who lived with his wife and family at the edge of a forest. Every day the woodcutter went to work deep in the forest, sometimes to cut down trees, sometimes to trim branches, sometimes to cut logs into firewood which he sold in the nearest town every market day.

The woodcutter was an honest, hard-working man, and although the family were not rich, they were happy and contented most of the time, and were certainly not starving.

One day the woodcutter was walking home after his day's work. He was tired and hungry and looking forward to his evening meal. The weather had been bad, there had been heavy rain during the day, and all the forest paths were wet and slippery. The woodcutter's route took him along the side of a fast flowing river, and suddenly, without knowing how it happened, the man's feet slipped from under him and he fell towards the water.

The woodcutter grabbed at overhanging tree branches and managed to save himself from falling into the river and drowning, but in his efforts to save himself, he let go of his axe. It disappeared into the swirling dark waters, and was lost.

'Oh no!' said the woodcutter. 'Now what am I going to do? Without my axe I can't work, and without work I can't earn money to feed my family. I'll have to try to get it back.' He held on tightly to the overhanging branches that had already saved him, and leaned out towards the water. He plunged his arm under the fast flowing surface of the river, but it was no good. The water was too deep, too fast, too dangerous, too cold, for him to have any chance of retrieving his axe.

But watching all this, was Mercury, one of the Gods. He knew the woodman to be a good man, and he decided to help. He suddenly appeared at the woodman's side, then dived into the dark racing water.

'Here!' he said, holding up an axe made of pure gold.. 'You dropped this I think. Have it back.'

'No. That's not mine,' said the woodcutter. 'I can't take that one. Mine is just an ordinary axe.'

'Then take this one,' said mercury, diving into the water again and emerging with a sparkling silver axe.

'But it's not mine,' said the honest woodcutter.

Mercury dived into the river again, and this time brought to the surface the woodcutter's own iron axe with its smooth wooden handle. The woodman smiled with pleasure.

'Oh thank you,' he said. 'I've worked with that axe for years, and no other one would seem the same. Thank you again.'

Mercury was so impressed with the honesty of the man, that he gave him the gold and silver axes in addition to his own.

'You deserve them,' he said. 'There aren't many honest people around these days.'

News of the woodcutter's luck soon reached his neighbours.

'Pity no luck ever comes *my* way,' grumbled one man. 'I don't see why he should have it all.' The man felt so aggrieved by the woodman's luck, he decided to see if the magic would work again, for him.

He, too, went deep into the forest. When he was far away from anyone who might see what he was doing, he threw his own axe into the middle of the river.

'Help me,' he shouted. 'Mercury, have pity on me. My axe has fallen into the river. I cannot work without it. Please come down and find it for me.'

In a trice Mercury had appeared. He dived into the water and held high a golden axe.

'Is this yours?' he asked.

'Oh yes. Yes. That's mine. I recognise it. That's mine all right. Thanks,' said the man.

'I think not,' said Mercury, as he dropped the golden axe back into the water. 'Dishonesty gets you nothing!' And he disappeared as suddenly as he had come, leaving the man standing at the edge of the river, able to see, but not reach, his own axe and the beautiful golden one, twinkling and sparking under the surface of the river.

In the days that followed, the man came often to the river, but was never able to regain either of the axes.

The mice in council

adapted from Aesop

Think before you speak

Once upon a time a family of mice lived in a large old house. They had lived there for many years, generation after generation, without any trouble or difficulty, until a cat moved in.

The cat was handsome and ginger, sure-footed and agile, intelligent and cunning. It was an excellent hunter. It stalked its victims silently, stealthily creeping closer and closer to them. It had the patience to wait, and wait, hidden for minutes, hours if necessary, until it judged exactly the right second to pounce. It never missed.

The family of mice grew smaller and smaller in number; the cat grew fatter and fatter.

At last the mice realised that if they were to stand any chance of surviving as a family, they would have to do something to stop the cat hunting them.

'We'll call a meeting,' they decided. 'We'll all meet together and decide what's to be done.'

They met at midnight, in the space behind the skirting board in the hallway. They were safe here. The entrance hole was too small to let the cat through. They started the meeting straight away, without delay. One of the older mice outlined the problem. The assembled mice agreed that something should be done. But what? They talked for an hour. Two hours. Then three. And four. But none of the suggestions was any good. None of the ideas would work. None of the mice could think of a way to stop the cat from hunting them.

Then, when they thought they'd discussed all the possibilities, one of the youngest mice spoke.

'I have an idea,' he said. 'We can't find a way to stop the cat hunting us. So what we need is a way of making sure we don't get caught.'

'Yes, that's right,' murmured all the mice.

'So we need a warning that he's coming. We need to be able to *hear* him coming, then we can escape.'

'That's it. That's right,' said the others.

'Why don't we hang a bell round his neck, then we'll hear him wherever he is. He won't be able to sneak up and surprise us, because we'll know where he is.'

'Brilliant idea,' cried the mice.

'Good thinking!'

'That's the best idea we've had all night.'

'Excellent,' they all said, and they all began talking at once, in high excited squeaking voices, because they were so pleased with the wonderful idea.

An old mouse, who had spent the entire meeting sitting near the back of the group, slowly and quietly got to his feet. He moved to the front of the crowd.

'It is a brilliant idea indeed,' he said. 'But I have a question. Tell me... who is going to hang the bell round the cat's neck?'

The meeting of mice grew silent. No-one spoke. No-one uttered a word. No-one knew the answer. But each of the mice knew that *they* were not going to be the one to put the bell on the cat.

'I thought so,' said the old mouse. 'Everyone wants the job to be done, but no-one wants to do it! It's no good having a brilliant idea if no-one is prepared to carry it out. It's easy to have a good idea, it's not so easy to put it into practice!'

The old mouse turned to the young mouse whose idea it was to put a bell round the cat's neck, 'Perhaps next time, you'll think through your idea before you speak it out loud,' he said. And he went away to his own mouse-hole under the stairs, leaving the meeting no further on than it had been at the beginning.

The milkmaid

Don't count your chickens/greed

adapted from La Fontaine

There was once a milkmaid, whose job it was to help a farmer look after, and milk, his herd of cows. Every week the girl was paid a wage for her work, and every week she was also given a large jug of milk. Sometimes she drank the milk. Sometimes she made it into butter. Once she made a creamy round cheese with it. Another time she made a milk pudding to eat. And on one occasion she shared it with a family of cats who lived in the cowsheds.

But one day, she took it to market to sell it. It was quite a way from her house to the market place, and she walked slowly, taking care not to spill a single drop of the milk. As she walked along, she began to think of what she would do with the money she'd get, when she sold the milk.

'It should sell easily,' she said to herself. 'It's good quality milk, clean and fresh. I should get a good price for it, even though there is only a jugful.

'When I get paid for it, I think I'll buy some hen's eggs. If I get a whole gold coin, I think I'll buy a hundred eggs. I'll hatch them out into chickens, and I'll look after the chickens, and rear them until *they* are big enough to sell at the market.

'Then I think I'll buy a pig. Yes, I'll buy a pig with the money I get from the chickens. I'll fatten it up, then sell it at the market. I'll get a really good price for a fine fat pig. I'll have serious money then!

'I'll have enough to buy a cow. In fact I'll probably have enough to buy two cows. They will be the start of my own herd of cows. I'll have as many cows in my herd as the farmer I work for. I'll have to find workers to help me, because there'll be too much work for me to do all by myself. I'll have to buy a bull. Then the cows can have calves. I'll need to buy a farm, with acres and acres of fields.

'I'll have a beautiful big farmhouse, and everyone will come from miles around to see me. I'll be able to invite all my friends and neighbours to dinner, and we'll have big parties out on the lawn in the summertime. I'll have beautiful gardens of course, and gardeners to look after them. I'll need servants and maids, butlers and cooks in my grand new house. Oh it will be *wonderful*!'

And the milkmaid gave a happy skip and a jump at the very thought of the wonderful life that lay ahead of her, just as soon as she had sold the jug of milk and could buy her first batch of eggs.

But the foolish milkmaid quite forgot that she was carrying the jug of milk that she was taking to market to sell. As soon as she skipped and jumped, the jug flew out of her hands and landed with a crash on the ground. She stared at the broken pieces of china, and at the white pool of milk which was fast disappearing into the cracks of the path.

She burst into angry tears as her dreams of chickens and pigs, cows and calves, beautiful farmhouses and parties on the lawn, and the wonderful life she was going to live, all disappeared down the footpath cracks, along with the spilt milk.

Sadly, she picked up the pieces of broken pottery and turned round to go home.

'Perhaps I shouldn't have made any plans until the milk was sold and I had the money,' she said. 'Perhaps I shouldn't have counted my chickens until they were hatched!'

This is one of the best examples of a traditional fable reaching the status of a proverb and entering into everyday language.

The crow and the swan   *Discontent/envy*
adapted from Aesop

There was once a fine healthy black crow, who was perfectly happy being himself, until he saw a swan. It was the first swan the crow had ever seen and he was amazed at how beautiful it was. The swan was swimming smoothly, slowly and majestically across the water towards another swan on the opposite side of the lake. They met, and stretched out their graceful necks towards each other. They gently touched one another with their orange beaks, and nudged each other with their heads. One of the swans slowly lifted its wings from its side and curved then over its back in an arch of white feathers.

'That's the most beautiful bird I've ever seen,' thought the crow. He looked down at his own black feathers, at his small size and at his short legs. 'How ugly I am,' he thought. He looked again at the swans, and in that instant, decided to be one.

He ran along the edge of the lake, picking up swans' feathers that had fallen to the ground. He collected quite a number, then stuck them in amongst his own black feathers. Then he jumped into the water and tried to swim about, just like the swans. He fished his wet wings out from his sides and held them up over his head, trying to copy the graceful arch the swan had made.

But somehow, none of this worked. He sank beneath the surface every time he tried to arch his wings. He couldn't swim in the same way as the swans, no matter how hard he tried. He splashed and spluttered, coughed and choked. Eventually he climbed out of the water and sat on the bank.

'I need practice,' he said. 'I can't expect to be a swan straight away. After all, they've been practising being themselves ever since they hatched out of their eggs. I must be patient, I must watch them, and I must try to do everything they do.'

So the crow moved in with the swans and copied everything they did. He swam when they swam, ate when they ate, slept when they slept, and generally practised behaving like them. But he didn't turn into a swan.

He tried harder. He scrubbed his feathers every day in the lake, in the hope that they would turn white more quickly. He practised swimming for eight hours each day instead of four. He gave up eating his usual food, and ate only the same food the swans ate. But he didn't turn into a swan.

By now the crow was beginning to look ill. He was exhausted from the constant swimming. His feathers were permanently water-logged, they were dull and lifeless. He was thin and weak with lack of proper food. His eyes were glazed and he had lost his voice. And he hadn't turned into a swan.

The swans began to tease him and make fun of him for trying to be like them. The ducks and geese on the lake advised him to give up trying to change into a swan, and go back simply to being himself. The crow looked down at his wet bedraggled feathers. 'Perhaps you're right,' he said. 'Perhaps it was a silly idea after all.'

He limped back to his old home and his old neighbours.

'I'm home. I've come...' he began. But he got no further. The crows that used to be his friends didn't recognise him. They beat this strange bird with their wings. They pecked at this curious creature with their beaks. They chased this odd-looking animal away, out of their neighbourhood.

'You're not one of us,' they called. 'Clear off! Go away! Find somewhere else!'

The crow crept away, hurt, disappointed, unwanted, unknown.

cf. La Fontaine's 'Crow and the peacock feathers'. In this parallel story a crow wants to become a peacock. He adorns himself with peacocks' tail feathers and struts about, only to be pecked almost to death by their owners. He tries to return to his flock, but is killed by them since they don't recognise him.

See also 'The foolish crow' page 25. The same theme is explored in La Fontaine's 'Crow and the eagle', and Aesop's 'The donkey and the dog', in which animals envy each other to the extent of wanting to become something they are not, with disastrous results.

The mouse, the cat and the cockerel   *Appearances can be deceptive*
adapted from La Fontaine

There was once a tiny mouse, who had been told by her mother to stay near their mousehole in the barn.

'You do not yet know the dangers there are in the world,' said the mother mouse. 'Stay near home. Don't go far away.'

For a while the young mouse did as she was told, but soon she became bored with staying still, with doing as she was told, with being good.

'I'm going exploring,' she said to herself, and she wandered away.

She crossed the barn and headed towards the open door. She stood in a shaft of sunlight and looked at the world beyond the barn. She saw a yard made of cobblestones. She saw a tall brown fence and a gate. She saw a large farmhouse, a line of washing blowing in the breeze, the farmer's wife going in through the kitchen door. And she saw a fat, furry, grey cat.

The cat was lying on a patch of rough grass by the back door of the farmhouse. It was resting its chin on its tucked in paws and watching the tiny mouse through half-closed eyes. The cat's sleek fur gleamed and shone in the sunlight. Its ears stood erect like tiny triangular satellite dishes, tuned in to the mouse's movements.

The mouse, who knew nothing of cats, never having seen one before, said 'What a beautiful animal. How still and quietly it sits. How bright and clean its fur is. I'd like to have that animal as my friend. I'll go and talk to it.'

She set off scurrying across the yard towards the grey cat, but no sooner had she gone a few steps, than a noisy cockerel came careering round the corner of the barn. It was huge compared with the small mouse. It had a bright red cockscomb on its head, and yellow feathers under its chin. It had enormous blue-green tail feathers curving behind it, and large brown speckled wings which it flapped until the dust on the farmyard floor rose up in clouds. It scratched and scraped at the ground with its clawlike feet and made the most alarming shrieking noise.

The mouse, who had never encountered a cockerel before, turned tail and fled back to the safety of the barn and her mousehole.

'Whatever's the matter with you?' asked her mother.

'I've just had the most dreadful fright,' said the tiny mouse. 'I've just seen the most dangerous creature. It was as big as a monster, and as scarey as a dragon. If I hadn't run away it would have eaten me. It was making the most horrible noise I've ever heard.'

'It was only a cockerel,' said her mother. 'It wouldn't have hurt you. It might look big and bold and frightening, but that's just its way. Cockerels don't eat mice, they peck the grain and grit from the farmyard floor. You shouldn't be scared of them.'

'Well I was,' answered the mouse. 'And now I'm cross, because I was on my way to talk to my friend when the cockerel scared me, and now he might have gone.'

'And who is your friend?' asked the mouse's mother.

'I don't know his name,' said the mouse. 'But he's beautiful. He has the smoothest fur and he looks gentle and kind. He was sitting in the sun and I could hear his voice; it was like the sound the tractor makes, but softer and quieter.'

'Now there's an animal to take care not to meet,' said the mother mouse. 'He might look quiet and well behaved, but he's a cat – the enemy of all our kind. It's lucky the cockerel came by when he did, or the cat would have pounced on you and killed you with one blow. Remember, the noisiest animals are not always the most dangerous, and the quietest ones are not always the safest. Appearances can be deceptive.'

The Travellers and the bear   *Loyalty*
adapted from Aesop

William and Henry were two good friends, who one day were travelling home together after visiting a town some distance from where they lived. They had been friends for a long time, they knew each other well, and were enjoying each other's company. They talked of this and that, they shared a joke, they laughed together.

But as they walked along, William kept turning round and looking behind him.

'What are you doing?' asked Henry.

'I keep thinking we're being followed,' said William, anxiously. 'I keep hearing a sound like footsteps, but every time I turn round, there's nothing to see.'

'I haven't heard anything,' said Henry.

They walked on a little further.

'There it is again,' said William. 'Can't you hear it?'

They both stopped and listened. There was no sound. Nothing to hear except a bird singing in a nearby tree. There was nothing to see. No-one on the road either in front or behind. No movement in the fields. Everything was still and quiet.

'It's eerie,' said William. 'It's too quiet. I'm sure there's something following us.'

Suddenly, out of the bushes at the side of the road, lumbered a huge brown bear. It reared up on its hind legs, as tall as a man. It stared at the two friends with blazing bright beady black eyes. The two men froze in terror where they stood.

'I know...' whispered Henry, quickly thinking of a plan to save them both. 'You move slowly...' but he had no time to say any more. William, without a thought for his friend, had taken to his heels and was running towards the tree at the side of the road.

'It's every man for himself,' he shouted. 'I'm going up this tree for safety. You can go where you want.'

The bear, angered by William's running and shouting, suddenly lunged forwards. Henry looked round him in panic for some safe place to go, but there was nowhere else to run. Nowhere else to go. William had taken the only place of safety there was, and he wasn't offering Henry any space in the tree.

Henry threw himself on the ground and lay perfectly still. He remembered reading somewhere that bears never attack a dead body. If he could make the bear think he was dead, perhaps he would save himself. He held his breath. He moved not a single muscle. He could hear the bear snuffling closer. He could smell the strong odour of its body. He could feel its closeness, but he dare not open his eyes to see what it was doing. He lay even more still.

The bear padded cautiously nearer and nearer to Henry. It sniffed around his face. It pawed at his arm and pulled it away from his body. It nudged its long nose underneath Henry, and tried to turn him over, but he fell back limply each time. The bear licked Henry's ear. It felt cool and still. The bear walked round Henry several times, but he never moved. The bear lost interest in this man who appeared to be dead, and it walked away.

For a long time afterwards, Henry continued to lie quite still. He was afraid to move in case the bear was still there, watching him, waiting to attack him. He knew he had had a very narrow escape from death. And he knew that his so-called friend William had done nothing to help him.

William, having watched the bear sniff round Henry then go away, climbed down from the safety of his tree.

'It's OK now,' he called. 'That was a good idea of yours to lie still and pretend to be dead. It worked, didn't it?'

'Yes, it worked,' said Henry quietly.

'It must have been scarey to lie there with that great bear sniffing round you,' said William. 'But tell me, what did it say to you? I saw it whisper something to you. I saw it with its mouth near your ear. What did it say?'

'It said I should be very careful who I choose to have as my friend!' said William. 'It said I should beware of people who say they are my friend, then only think of themselves when there is danger!' And William got up from the ground, and went home the rest of the way by himself.

cf. 'The woodpecker, the tortoise and the antelope', page 16, in which the friends are loyal and true to each other, risking their own lives in order to save each other.

The pigeon and the ant   *Loyalty/one good turn deserves another*
adapted from La Fontaine

Once upon a time, an ant was busy searching for food at the edge of a stream, when she missed her footing and fell into the water. The stream, which was shallow and safe for other creatures, was a dangerous raging torrent to one as small as the ant, and she was in imminent danger of drowning.

Luckily, flying overhead, just at the moment when the ant fell into the stream, was a wood pigeon. He saw the danger the ant was in, so flew to the nearest tree, picked off a leaf with his beak, flew back to the ant, and dropped the leaf so that it fell to the water near enough for the ant to reach.

She struggled onto it and lay half-dead on its surface, gasping for air. The leaf floated downstream like a life-boat and eventually was washed against the mud at the side of the stream. The ant, now feeling better and stronger, climbed off the leaf, clambered up the muddy bank away from the water, and reached the safety of the grass. She looked up into the trees and said 'Thank you wood pigeon, if you're listening. I owe you my life. I'll not forget you, and one day I may be able to save your life in return.'

The wood pigeon heard the ant's voice, but laughed as he flew away, high into the sky. 'I appreciate your thanks little ant,' he said. 'But forget it! You're too small to be able ever to save my life,' and he swooped down low over the stream, before soaring again above the treetops, just to prove how big and brave and clever and strong he was, compared to the tiny ant.

But, two days later the wood pigeon was no longer laughing. He was flying for his life, trying to escape a boy with a bow and arrow.

'Pigeon pie!' shouted the boy, as he took arrow after arrow out of the quiver on his back, and took aim at the wood pigeons. The boy had already killed several birds and had stuffed them into a sack by his feet.

'Just another one,' he said. 'Then I'll have enough. They'll make a good pie for my tea tonight. Just another one.'

He pulled another arrow from the quiver. The wood pigeon, hiding in the branches of the tree above the boy's head could see the sharpened point on the end of the arrow. He could see the feathers on the end of the shaft that made the arrow fly straight and true. Straight and true to the target, for the boy was a good shot and rarely missed his aim.

The boy could see the wood pigeon. The tree's leaves were partly hiding the bird, but the boy knew exactly where it was. He fitted the arrow to the string of his bow. He took aim and pulled the bowstring back along the length of his arm. Back and back towards his shoulder until the bow was bent as far as it would go and the arrow was lined up straight and sure. All the time he kept his eye on the wood pigeon.

'Now!'

But in that second when the boy was about to release the bowstring and send the arrow flying to the heart of the wood pigeon, he felt a sharp pain in his ankle.

'Ow!' He dropped the arrow and his bow, and looked down at his ankle. A bite! A large red ant bite on his ankle! He rubbed the swelling, then picked up his bow and arrow again, to take aim at the wood pigeon.

'Just another one,' he said. 'That's all I need. Just another one to make enough for pigeon pie for my tea.'

But when the boy looked up into the canopy of leaves, the wood pigeon had gone. It soared away into the sky. 'Thank you ant,' it said. 'I thought you were too small to be able to save my life, but I was wrong. Thank you for your loyalty.'

cf. Aesop's 'Lion and the Mouse', in which a lion agrees to release a mouse, but refuses to believe that the mouse might one day save him in return. Later, the lion becomes trapped in a net and the mouse releases him by gnawing through the threads.

See also 'The woodpecker, the tortoise and the antelope' on page 16, and 'The travellers and the bear' on page 154, which also explore the theme of loyalty and friendship.

The birds, the beasts and the bat   *Loyalty*
adapted from Aesop

Once, a long time ago, the birds and the animals were at war. They could not agree on who should live where, or who should eat what, on who should be in charge or who should not. They had the fiercest arguments and the most dreadful fights. There was hardly a day went by but that some creature was not injured or killed.

Sometimes it seemed that the animals were winning the battles. They would lie in wait until the birds were eating or sleeping, then rush in and attack them. The birds tried posting look-outs to watch for raids, but somehow the animals always surprised them.

At other times the birds seemed to be winning. They too would wait until the animals were off-guard, sleeping or eating, but their attacks were always from the air. They would swoop down from the treetops or sky, always in line with the sun so that their enemy could not see them clearly. Then they would peck with their beaks at the faces of the surprised animals.

One creature however, was always on the winning side, never with the losers. He was the bat. He was in a unique position of course, for he had the body of an animal, but he also had wings and could fly. He constantly changed his mind as to which side he was on, depending on who was winning at the time. When the birds were apparently doing well, the bat became one of them and fought on their side. But when the situation reversed and the animals emerged on top, he stopped being a bird and joined the animals.

At last the war ended. The differences were settled, the arguments ended, the fighting stopped and peace was restored between birds and animals. There had been too many hurt, too many injured, too many killed, for the war to continue.

'Enough is enough,' they all said. 'We must learn to live in harmony in the world that we share.'

The bat was pleased that the war was over. 'Now everyone will be my friend,' he thought. 'They will *all* know how much I contributed to the war. After all, I must be the only animal that was on both sides. They'll all be pleased with me. In fact I'll probably be welcomed as a hero. They may want to have a special celebration for me, a wonderful end-of-war-party to thank me for all I did for the animals *and* the birds,' and the bat smiled to himself at the thought of the splendid times ahead.

He was therefore rather surprised when things didn't turn out as he thought they would. Far from being greeted like a hero, he discovered that the animals wanted nothing to do with him. 'We don't want you here,' they said. 'You're nothing but a traitor. You were not fighting on our side, you were on the side of the birds.'

'No I wasn't!' said the bat. 'At least not all the time. I was on your side as well.'

'That's just it!' said the animals. 'You changed your mind. You kept swapping sides. You were hypocritical. You were pretending to be on whichever side was winning at the time. Well we don't like that. Go away!'

The bat felt all this was very unfair, but said 'Well, see if I care. I'll go and join the birds. They'll want me. They'll know how helpful I was in the war.'

But the bat received the same response from the birds.

'Traitor!' they shouted. 'You were loyal to no-one. You didn't help either the animals or us. You let us all down. The only person you were interested in saving was yourself. We want nothing to do with you. Go away!'

And from that day to this, the bat has been a species apart, ignored by both the animals and the birds of the world.

The frogs and their king   *Discontent/appearances can be deceptive*
adapted from Aesop

There was once a huge colony of frogs living in a large pond. They'd lived there for years, untroubled by anyone else, free to do as they chose.

One day the frogs grew bored, restless, dissatisfied.

'Every day is always the same,' they said. 'Nothing different ever happens here. Nothing new ever happens. We need things to liven up a little. We need a king to lead us, to guide us, to show us what to do.'

The frogs appealed to the god Jupiter. 'Please send us a king,' they said. 'We need a king of our own.'

Jupiter was amused at the frogs' request. 'I'll send you a king,' he laughed. 'I'll send you a great and mighty king, the likes of which you've never seen before!' And Jupiter threw an enormous log into the centre of the frogs' pond. It landed with a splash which sent the startled frogs leaping and swimming to find a safe place to hide.

The log lay half submerged under the water. The frogs peeped out from their hiding places and stared at it, not realising what it was.

'He doesn't say much, does he?' said one frog.

'I expect he's waiting for us,' said another.

'Hello King,' said several frogs all at once.

There was no reply from the log.

'He doesn't look much like a king,' said one.

'But we didn't say what the king had to look like,' said someone else.

'No, but I didn't think he would look like that,' said the first frog.

The frogs by now had all gathered round their new king. They were unsure what they should do next, never having had a king before. They talked in hushed voices.

'Do you think he's asleep?' asked one.

'You don't think he's *dead* do you,' said another. 'He might have hit his head when he landed in the pool.'

The frogs felt alarmed at this possibility, and decided that one of them should poke the king to see if he was alive. They pushed the largest frog forward.

'Go on,' they said. 'Touch him.'

The big frog cautiously poked the log with his strong hind leg. The log moved a little and settled more firmly on the bottom of the pond.

'He's alive,' said the frog. 'He moved, so he must be alive.'

By now some of the younger frogs had also touched the new king. When they realised that he was not going to tell them off, or get angry with them, they became braver and bolder. They climbed on the king's back and used him as a diving board. They swam round him and under him, forgetting that they had been scared of him only a few minutes earlier.

Soon all the frogs were using the new king in whatever way they wanted. The older frogs were climbing up onto his back for their afternoon sleep. The mother frogs were using him to teach the baby frogs their first wobbly jumps. The youngsters were sunbathing on him, or diving from him, or chasing each other up and down along his back. But after a few days of this, the frogs grew bored again.

'We wanted a king who would *do* something,' they said. 'This king does nothing at all. He lets us do just what we want, but we used to do that anyway. What's the point of having a king, if he doesn't order us around?'

So the frogs appealed once more to the god Jupiter.

'We need a better king,' they said. 'Someone who will *do* something. Someone who will be a bit more active.'

'The trouble with you, is that you're never satisfied,' said Jupiter, crossly. 'You don't know when you are well off! You should be content with what you have. But... if you want a king who is a bit more active... I'll give you one!'

And without further ado, Jupiter sent a stork to the frogs' pool. It was tall and elegant, with a huge wingspan and a long sharp pointed beak.

'Now this is more like a king,' said the frogs.

'Welcome, Your Majesty.'

'We're pleased to have you join us.'

'Long live our new king,' they said.

But the frogs' pleasure was short lived. Oh, the new king was active enough. Active in eating frogs for supper. Active in chasing them round the pond for sport. Active in digging them out of the mud with its long beak. Active in killing them.

'Please give us back our old king,' they said to Jupiter. 'Please take this new one away.'

But Jupiter said 'No. A good master may not be appreciated until he's replaced by a bad one. You should have been content with what you had.'

Further reading

Aesop's Fables Graeme Kent (Brimax Books Ltd 1991)
Fables for our Time & More Fables for our Time James Thurber (Mandarin Paperbacks 1991)
La Fontaine's Fables Diana Athill (Andre Deutsch 1984)
Medieval Fables – Marie de France Jeanette Beer (Dragon's World Ltd 1981)
The Best of Aesop's Fables Margaret Clarke & Charlotte Voake (Walker Books)
World Fables Yong Yap Cotterell (Book Club Associates 1979)

Alphabetical index of stories

(Letters in brackets refer to the religious background from which the stories come. B = Buddhism, C = Christianity, H = Hinduism, I = Islam, J = Judaism, P = Primal religions, S = Sikhism, T = Traditional western fables)

Index of stories
by religious background

Theme index

(Letters in brackets refer to the religious background from which the stories come. B = Buddhism and so on.)